Abu El Banat

Father of Daughters

by Dolah Saleh

PublishAmerica
Baltimore

First printing

ISBN: 1-60672-547-5
PUBLISHED BY PUBLISHAMERICA, LLLP
www.publishamerica.com
Baltimore

Printed in the United States of America

For my dear father with dcep gratitude and everlasting love.

Introduction

Everyone knows the story of the single mom. And today, we all realize that there is such a thing as a single dad. Still, in the 1950s, one might have been hard pressed to find an immigrant father with a swing shift job raising five children on his own. Here is one father's story and how he became responsible for five children ultimately resolving their feelings toward their own "absent" mother, the object of their youthful discontent.

The backdrop is labor and blue-collar work of the booming 1950s, an unhappy marriage five kids later, the grief of separation and the things missed about being a family intact. It is about not fitting in, about the experience of feeling between races and religions, straddling Christian and Moslem traditions. It is about learning the lessons of sacrifice and unconditional love in an often scary world of discrimination and rebellion.

******

The day I decided to write this book I knew it would necessitate reliving a number of unpleasant memories. I questioned the value of what I understood would be a cathartic experience. Still, the more I thought about it, the more I knew that the story of a Yemenite Arab who ended up in America raising four daughters (an unenviable position in his culture) and a son, all of whom grew up to be contributing members of society, was a story worth telling.

"Papa" was an immigrant who took on a great deal as a single father in the innocent yet transitional 50's and the turbulent 60's—

when major public figures were assassinated and the country was being dragged into a controversial and protracted war in most foreign territory. By the time the 70s had arrived, Papa had five teenagers and America was well into social upheaval and a sexual revolution. It was a time of civil unrest, a seizing drug and hippie counter culture, and a palpable loss of confidence in our national government.

This book pays tribute to one man's ability to maintain dignity and a semblance of family against all odds in a most unlikely situation. Life in his new country with his American-born children was not only the biggest challenge of his trailblazing life, but he would bear it with principle, a sense of humor, and perhaps just enough naiveté to not scare him into submission. Today I believe that those times taught his family the most important lessons in life, lessons that transcend time. His legacy is the gift of wisdom he left with each of his five grateful children.

I a "Normal" Family

As a child, I used to pray to God every night that my mom would come home and we could have a "normal" family. As I grew up, I used to pray that my father would return home safe from work and not die since he was much older than my friends' fathers,...and then I just prayed that we would all survive the chaos.

I used to watch him sleep. Monitoring the steady cadence of each breath, I sought routine reassurance in momentary stops in my playtime to watch for the undulation of his chest as proof that he rests. I have no reason to fear for now, *not this moment*, I would tell myself.

Other kids had fathers in their thirties. Ours was in his sixties. But he could not be allowed to die. Among other horrible thoughts, there was the looming threat that the five of us are off to Father Baker's Home, where we would likely be separated into several different homes. Papa would never let that happen. He has to live until we are all adults and have independent lives of our own.

My vigilance grew with each passing year. When he was really in a sound, peaceful sleep, his cheeks inflated and then slowly deflated in a steady rhythmic pattern. *Just a second,* I would have to check. Then, relaxed enough to continue with whatever I was doing—*Ok, let's go*.

I used to think that my odd private practice was unique until one day I heard my sister say that she had developed a similar enduring habit. At the time, no one could admit or express that we worried about our father leaving us while we were still too young and not ready to be without him. For us, life without Papa was just too difficult to even imagine.

From as far back as I can remember, I was consciously aware of our difference. My three sisters, my brother and I were being raised by our father, *not* our mother. Our father was a foreigner, an Arab, and most people did not even know what that was. *"Do you wear that red jewel in the middle of your forehead?"* kids asked us. Once understood, the children would quickly resort to calling us "camel jockeys." Even with a Muslim father, however, we had been baptized Catholic by our mother, a fact that would cause great family controversy and eventually become an ongoing source of confusion. We lived in a neighborhood predominately inhabited by those of Polish, Italian and Irish decent where almost everyone had fair skin and smooth hair. We had neither.

The trouble with being different when you're a kid is that you really do want to be like everyone else. Fitting in is desirable, indeed imperative. Even the way other children referred to their parent was not as we did. We had asked if we could call our father "Dad" to be like our friends, but he flatly refused to allow it. This was strictly an "American term" and with that explanation you got the feeling it was somehow less than respectful. "Abu" is the Arabic word for father, and "Baba" the way you referred to him. Our Americanized version became "Papa."

Fitting in was never going to be easy for a family who was difficult to categorize in the first place. We were latch key kids before the term existed. Our mother was alive and around, but she was not at home waiting for us with dinner like the Leave-It-To-Beaver mothers of the time. *At least that was the preoccupation occurring in my young self-consciousness back then.* Our darker skin and general look stirred many a sideward glance and our long, thick, curly hair was always a major source of anxiety and frustration for us four girls. Even though we would attempt every trick in the book to get our hair to look like our girlfriends', we settled for braids and ringlets for a measure of control and these were styles that did not exactly make for fashionable hairdos. We were un-streetwise kids living in a city neighborhood where it was becoming more challenging with each passing day. The fact that we attended a Catholic institution only added to our Milquetoast reputation, especially among the 'heathens' at the public schools.

Life in Buffalo, New York

We lived at 66 Myrtle Avenue, a city street in Buffalo, New York with homes, apartment buildings, and factories all in one block. The neighborhood was friendly; people and storeowners were on a first name basis. We even had running tabs with two local grocery stores so that we could go and get anything we needed without the cash, especially when Papa was working his day or early evening shift.

"Jackie's store" was on Seneca Street and only a thirty second run from our front door through an empty lot, but the old store was wide and deep and took a prominent position on the block with a narrow sidewalk separating it from the street. Jackie was a dark-haired heavy-set American Indian lady who liked Papa alright but was only haltingly nice to the droves of us kids who frequented her store. At one point, she took to limiting the number of patrons under age 18 who could enter at one time. Her store enticed us with a great selection of three-for-a-penny candy and tempting chocolate bars that sat inside a large clear glass cabinet. On the counter, a jar of huge pickles, sold for a few cents a piece. The entire first floor of the building was mostly enclosed with huge glass windows and double glass doors contained in distressed wood frames that allowed a clear view inside. A small bell announced your entry onto the worn hard wood floors with crevices in particular traffic patterns around the store. There were shelving units that sat on either side as you entered, containing basic dry goods. Jackie kept the store open long hours, perhaps because all she had to do was take a few steps up into her attached flat in the back of the building.

Usually on a Friday, pay day, Papa was prepared to settle his debts.

Yaa Jeckie, how much I owe?

Papa always began his address of a person with the Arabic term, *Yaa,* and somehow mispronounced everyone's name, if only just a little. But he always paid his bills, fully and on time; no one ever concerned themselves with his credit reliability. And since I don't remember him ever admonishing us on the amount, we must have done a good job of keeping our weeklong purchases within reasonable limits. Anyway, Jackie would have the handwritten running tallies, announce the total turning the notebook page toward Papa for his verification, and he would obligingly lay out the cash. While they settled, Papa asked about the family...always asked about the family...*how is this one or that one, how's the dok or cat,* if they had a pet. He might make some other small talk and perhaps purchase a pack of cigarettes. And that may be accomplished with some friendly haggling as there were occasional barters now and again, based on some appreciation of the fact that Papa was considered a good "regular" customer.

Lorigo's store was on Swan Street, a whole five-minute walk in the opposite direction, with Myrtle Avenue in between and parallel to both Seneca and Swan. Mr. Lorigo, or simply "Lorigo," as Papa called him, was a small olive-skinned Italian man who wore dark-rimmed glasses that were too big for his small structured face. My sister remembers him as a rather nervous type with such rapid speech that one was left with the impression he wanted his patrons to hurry, get what they needed and leave. Perhaps just another store owner's prerogative to shoo pesky children away. The busy store was a sprawling ranch-style that sat in between a two story wood apartment building and a regular single family home near the corner of Michigan Avenue. It too had worn hardwood floors with jam-packed shelves and counter tops. There was a deli section to one side where one could purchase a variety of luncheon meats. When Papa showed up at least once each week to pay our tab, which was a larger one than at Jackie's due to greater quantity and variety of food products, we got to see a lighter side of Mr. Lorigo. His downstate accent was charming and I remember thinking that perhaps that was what he and my father had in common as they seemed to take their time chatting whenever Papa came in to the store.

Myrtle Avenue was so close to downtown that we would walk to do our shopping, visit the main post office, pay utility bills (Papa paid each bill by personal visit and in cash only) and attend the annual St. Patrick's Day parade. An appealing city neighborhood in the 1950s, it had begun to deteriorate by the start of the new decade. Mom had said that all the "good people" were frightened away by the unsavory characters moving *in*. As a child, I was left to wonder why that happened and didn't really understand what my mother meant by *all the good people*.

Buffalo was a city that enjoyed great prominence at the turn of the century, good times steadily increasing to actually peak in the 1950s. Folks who were there at the time say that it was the place to be in the 1950s, the same decade during which all five of us were born. Canadians from Toronto would come across the border to Buffalo for entertainment and shopping. Today that trend is quite reversed. Looking back now, it seems to have been an innocent time for a city that was bustling with activity. And not unlike other American cities at the time, one gets a sense that there was a safety and security back then that does not exist today.

There were 580,000 people living in Buffalo—almost twice as many as there are today. It was the fifteenth largest city in the United States with a tavern for every 600 residents. People shopped downtown at family-owned department stores and viewed the latest films at local cinemas on Main Street. The 1950s were a time preceding suburban sprawl, so most community events were urban-centered.

For leisure, we children read comic books and watched *Leave it To Beaver* and *I Love Lucy* on television or played all kinds of street games in front of our homes. Kick ball and tag and hopscotch were constant favorites among the numerous neighborhood children, all of ages similar to my sisters, my brother and me and most of whom attended the same Catholic school we did.

I can't remember not having a television but I do recall that there were set "times" for watching, according to Papa. We had to get our dinner and homework done first, laundry, if we had it, and then, usually as a family, we sat and watched TV. Papa enjoyed many programs, especially programs that showcased musical talents so we regularly tuned into the *Ed Sullivan* and *Lawrence Welk* shows. *Bonanza*, or "Bonana," as he pronounced it, was his preference for dramatic series, perhaps because he was impressed with the story lines that clearly demonstrated strong family values.

Jimmy Durante was Papa's all-time favorite TV personality. Actually, it was between him and Danny Thomas. We all teased him, saying that it was because he, Mr.Thomas and Mr. Durante all shared the same nose, and he laughed in his self-deprecating way. Papa, like Danny, had what is commonly known as a typical Lebanese nose and it wasn't until many years later that I would realize that Jimmy Durante was actually Italian and not Lebanese at all.

News and History

Papa was kind of a news junky, so in addition to listening to daily reports on the regular house radio, he kept a short-waved radio right by his bedside, tuned to the station that discussed worldly news events, especially those that involved the Middle East.

Listen...he would whisper loudly, placing an attentive ear to his beloved static-seized short-wave broadcast as he assiduously kept informed of any detail on the conflict of his people.

Wait, wait...He pointed an upright index finger midair in our direction, signaling all activity and chatter to cease at once.

Listen, I say... urging his children to be as interested as he was in current events around the globe. And there was a lot going on, particularly right here in the States where Papa decided to stay and make his lifelong home.

It was a dichotomous environment in many ways, with art's innocence attesting to the fact that it had yet to catch up with life's brutal national and global realities. We may have been watching the silly antics of Lucille Ball on her weekly show but serious and deadly dramas were unfolding all around us.

I can recall Papa's sadness in the 1960s about the Six-Day War and ensuing problems in Arab lands, although at the time I hardly understood what all that really meant. Still, he celebrated the formation of the People's Democratic Republic of (South) Yemen in November 1967. The 1960s in the United States were challenging also, beginning with the threat of nuclear war during the Missile Crisis in 1962, the death of a beloved President in 1963 and ending with racial riots and the assassinations of two politically revered men, Robert Kennedy and Martin Luther King, Jr.. Vietnam was the hated war. Papa's only son was too young to be called, but my parents knew other people's sons who had been drafted and served. One young man, a family friend who was close to my older sister, was killed sometime in the late 1960s.

******

Papa was immersed in city life in America, but he was from such a different world. The rural highlands of Yemen had to feel like a lifetime departure, especially after so many years in America. He was from a small village called Mahakara, in the northeast part of Yemen, *on the other side of the mountain*, I was told by a close family friend from a village in the same general area, *Ibb*. We can locate Ibb on the map of Yemen, but Mahakara is not marked. His family's livelihood was sheep. Papa talked a lot about herding sheep and the mountains of Yemen, not an area of significant oil reserves and therefore not directly involved in many of the ongoing conflicts. The climate is very hot and dry and the desert harsh. It is said that the life expectancy was about 59.83 years of age and that there is an average of seven children born to each woman. Male literacy at my father's time was about fifty-three percent.

What began as a job assignment on an English ship out of Aden would end in a life changing decision for Papa. As he stopped at the diverse ports of call in various countries, including America on more than one occasion, at one point he decided to get off in New York City and stay. It is unclear whether he had been planning on it from the start, but since he was an employee of the ship and Yemen was still a British protectorate (his passport reported his "nationality" as British), he may have been scheduled to return to England. But this was an adventurous and daring young man whose defiant independence would sometimes get him into tight spots. He expressed pride over those kinds of accomplishments, too. In his view, it was necessary at times to "fool" (with) people, especially rule-insistent authorities whose regulations were unnecessarily harsh.

Nationality Certificate.

(Before this Document can be accepted as evidence of nationality, the following Certificate must be signed by a Superintendent of Mercantile Marine Office and his Official Stamp placed against his signature.)

After examining the Documents of the Bearer, I hereby certify that I am satisfied that he is a ______ subject.

Signature ______

Official Stamp

Stamps *of other* *Governments.*

Date of Birth ______ (Day) ______ (Month) 1876 (Year)

Place of Birth Aden (Town) ______ (Country)

Nationality British

Nationality of Father British

Height 5/13 Colour of Hair Dark Eyes Dark

Tattoo and other distinguishing marks: ______

PHOTOGRAPH.

LEFT THUMB PRINT.
Compulsory in the case of Asiatics, Africans and other coloured seamen.

14 MAR 1922

IMMIGRATION OFFICER (14) 10 NOV 1922 LIVERPOOL

Papa's early passport

Papa often told about his adventure and initial arrival into New York through Ellis Island when at some point he had to face rather rigorous questioning to determine his physical and mental health as entry prerequisite at that time. It was a good demonstration of his wit and ability to outsmart the authorities, although he likely was not getting away with much. He carried on in this way in an effort to parry his concerns and mistrust in a disadvantageous situation. He would tell the story:

What you name? they ask me.

Yes. I say.

How old you?

Yes.

Where you from?

Yes. I say again.

He had to have been generally healthy, he was definitely young, and so the thought was that he "passed" on the basis of visual observation and assumed promise. Papa laughed about this for years after because he indeed had understood enough English to answer the officers' questions, had practiced on the ships every chance he got but decided it was better not to take any chances since he was unsure what the "correct" answers actually were.

كيف تتكلم الإنجليزية
في أربعة أيام بدون معلم

How to speak ENGLISH
without a Teacher in 4 days.

دائما تذكروا...؟
منتجات شركة الشمرلى
ظروف . جوابات . بلوك نوت . يوميات
نوت . دفاتر تجارى . كراسات
محاضرات . مطبوعات
ماركة الفائز

كذلك منتجاتها السنوية
أجندات عربية وأفرنكية . نتائج حائط هجرية وميلادية
مفكرات يوم ويومين . نتائج جيب

اقرأ...؟
يوم الأربعاء
من كل أسبوع
مجلتك المحبوبة
«علي بابا»
مجلة الأدب والثقافة والقصص
والمغامرات والمسابقات المصورة
وتصدر عن دار
شركة الشمرلى للطبع والنشر

English	Arabec	إنجليزي	عربي
Signal	Esharah	سجنال	إشارة
Taxi Cab	Taxi	تاكسي كب	تكسي
The Fare	El-Ograh	ذي فير	الأجرة
Waiter	Garson	ويتر	جارسون
Bag	Shantah	بج	شنطة
The Payment	El-Dafea	ذي پيمنت	الدفع

الاصطلاحات العسكرية : مليتيري تيرمس
Military Terms : Isstlahat Asskariya

Liet. General	Fereek	ليوتانت جنرال	فريق
Colonel	Amiralai	كولونيل	أميرالاي
Liet. Colonel	Kaeimakam	ليوتانت كولونيل	قائمقام
Major	Sagh	ميجور	صاغ
Captain	Yozbashi	كابتن	يوزباشي
Lietenant	molazem awel	ليتانت	ملازم أول
2nd Lietenant	Molazem Tani		ملازم ثاني
SergentMajor	Sol Talim	سرجنت ميجور	صول تعليم
Sergent	Sol Tayeen	سرجنت	صول تعيين

(تم الكتاب)
الترجمان المفيد
يعلمك بدون معلم، بطريقة سهلة جدا
اللغة العربية، والإنجليزية، والإفرنسية

Papa's small and handy little booklet bound by black sewing thread: How to Speak English Without a Teacher in 4 Days

I think now that if they had not passed him with this tack, he might have suddenly been capable of defending his entry in another manner. Papa's inventive nature would no doubt offer an immediate alternate strategy. After all, he had been honing his resourcefulness from an early age when he first decided to leave his homeland in search of a new life.

According to historical documents that I found during my research, there are many Salehs who came to America from Arab lands. It's not surprising, given the fact that it is a common family name. There are three whose names are very close to Papa's, two with the spelling of Hayam, and another, Hassam, each sailing from the English ports of either Liverpool or Newcastle upon Tyne. All arrived in Ellis Island on a ship called "The Bradford City" in 1922 at 25 or 26 years of age and all were marked "members of the ship's crew." The records I uncovered noted that these men all worked on ships as fitters or firemen.

Papa had told us that he worked as both and learned to be a cook and medic also, although the last two positions could have been on different ships. It appears as though he worked as a crew member on many different ships in order to finally arrive in the United States and he spoke of many countries he visited, such as Brazil, as well as other places in South America and Europe. I was only able to find his personal paperwork for the English boat, *the Bradford City*. Since Papa's signature always made the "z" in his name look like one or even two "S's," or even a "y," I assume they had him listed as such and I never found any names with what I could make out as with the "z" spelling, Haziam, which is the one he actually used.

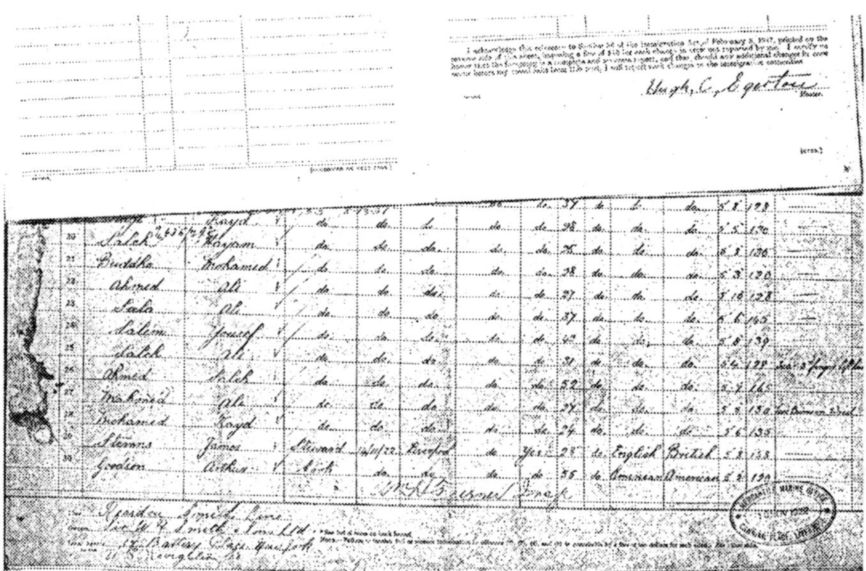

Papa is entered on log as #10, "Hayam," on ship manifest.

Sheet No. 1

LIST OR MANIFEST OF ALIENS EMPLOYED ON THE VESSEL AS MEMBERS OF CREW 189

Required [illegible] February 5, 1917, to be delivered to the United States immigration officer by the representatives of any vessel having such aliens on board upon arrival at a port of the United States.

Vessel S.S. Bradford City arriving at New York December 8, 192[illegible] from the port of Liverpool

No. on list	Family name	Given name	Position in ship's company	Shipped or engaged: When	Shipped or engaged: Where	Whether to be paid off or discharged at port of arrival	Whether able to read	Age	Sex	Race	Nationality	Height	Weight	Physical marks or peculiarities
1	Egerton	Hugh Charles	Master	14/11/27	Liverpool	No	Yes	42	Male	English	British	5.6	156	—
2	Burgess	Percy W.	1st Mate	do	do	do	do	26	do	do	do	5.9	160	—
3	Randall	Thomas R.	2nd do	do	do	do	do	53	do	do	do	6.0	172	—
4	Masters	Cecil H.	3rd do	do	do	do	do	23	do	do	do	5.8	154	—
5	Clarke	Samuel	Carpenter	do	do	do	do	50	do	English	British	5.10	158	—
6	Wylie	Anthony	Bosun	do	do	do	do	23	do	Scotch	British	5.9	160	—
7	Buckingham	Lionel A.	AB	do	do	do	do	20	do	English	British	5.6	170	—
8	Mouat	John	do	do	do	do	do	26	do	Scotch	do	5.10	167	—
9	Hoye	Frank	do	do	do	do	do	49	do	English	do	5.7	161	—
10	Grey	Roger	do	do	do	do	do	41	do	do	do	5.6	140	—
11	Spaik	Joseph	do	do	do	do	do	35	do	do	do	5.9	158	—
12	Brooky	Harrison	1st Engr.	do	do	do	do	56	do	English	British	5.6	140	—
13	Sanderson	Ivor M.	2nd do	do	do	do	do	29	do	do	do	5.7	144	—
14	Westgarth	Leslie W.	3rd do	do	do	do	do	25	do	do	do	5.8	152	—
15	Hayton	Roberts	4th do	do	do	do	do	36	do	do	do	5.5	170	—
16	Ali	Abdul	Donkeyman	do	do	do	Arabic	34	do	British Indian	do	5.4	130	—
17	Hassan	Mohamed	Fireman	do	do	do	do	26	do	do	do	5.4	130	
18	Abdullah	Mohamed	do	do	do	do	do	37	do	do	do	5.8	128	—
19	Nagi	Hayd	do	do	do	do	do	28	do	do	do	5.5	130	
20	Saleh	Hayam	do	do	do	do	do	35	do	do	do	5.8	130	
21	Fuddlla	Mohamed	do	do	do	do	do	28	do	do	do	5.3	120	
22	Ahmed	Ali	do	do	do	do	do	27	do	do	do	5.10	123	
23	Sala	Ali	do	do	do	do	do	37	do	do	do	5.6	145	
24	Salem	Yousef	do	do	do	do	do	40	[illegible]	[illegible]	do	5.8	139	
25	Saleh	Ali	[illegible]	do	do	do	do	31	do	[illegible]	do	5.4	139	[illegible]
26	Khaid	Saleh	do	do	do	do	do	57	do	do	do	5.7	165	
27	Mohamed	Ali	do	do	do	do	do	27	do	do	do	5.5	130	[illegible]
28	Mohamed	Hayd	do	do	do	do	do	27	do	do	do	5.6	135	
29	Stevens	James	Steward	14/11/27	Liverpool	do	Yes	58	do	English	British	5.8	143	
30	Gordon	Arthur	Cook	do	do	do	do	55	do	American	American	5.5	120	

Papa's entry here is #20

Entry on Line #28

Aug Nov
1914-18 WWI
1939-45 WWII

EXTRACT FROM IMMIGRATION ACT OF FEBRUARY 5, 1917

STATEMENT OF MASTER OF VESSEL REGARDING CHANGES IN CREW PRIOR TO DEPARTURE. 186

U. S. DEPARTMENT OF LABOR
IMMIGRATION SERVICE

Port of New York
9 December 1922

I, master of the British S.S. Bradford City from port of Liverpool hereby notify that the following is a complete record of all changes in the personnel of the crew of said vessel since arrival at this port:

Total crew at time of arrival 39 Number of seamen deserted 1

Number of seamen discharged ——— Seamen left in hospital (or died) ———

Number of seamen signed on at this port ——— Total crew this date 38

The above-named vessel arrived at this port 8 December, 1922, consigned to U.S. Navigation Co Inc is now lying at 16 Gray Bay and is expected to sail 19 Dec 1922, for Philadelphia via United States port of ——— First port of call in United States this voyage was New York.

Following is a detailed and accurate statement of all changes in crew:

DESERTING SEAMEN.

	Name.	Age.	Nationality.	Where and when signed on.
(20)	Hayam Salel	25	Arabian	Liverpool 19/11/22

Dis. 1

CERTIFICATE OF DISCHARGE

FOR A SEAMAN DISCHARGED BEFORE A SUPERINTENDENT OR A CONSULAR OFFICER.

ISSUED BY THE BOARD OF TRADE.

No. 28

Name of Ship and Official Number, Port of Registry and Tonnage.	*Horse Power.*	*Description of Voyage or Employment.*
Bradford City. 140887. Bideford. 3173.	517.	U.S.A.

Name of Seaman.	*Year of Birth.*	*Place of Birth.*
Hayam Saleh.	1897.	Aden.

Rank or Rating.	*No. of R.N.R. Commission or Certif.*	*If Mate or Engineer, No. of Cert. (if any).*
Fireman & Trimmer.	----	---

Date of Engagement.	*Place of Engagement.*
27/6/22.	Poplar.
Date of Discharge.	*Place of Discharge.*
23/8/22.	Poplar.

Copy of Report of Character. — *For Ability.* | *For General Conduct.*

I certify *that the above particulars are correct and that the named Seaman was discharged accordingly.**

Dated this 23 *day of* Aug. 1922

.... MASTER.

AUTHENTICATED BY

.... Signature of Superintendent

* If the Seaman does not require a Certificate of his character, enter "Endorsement" ... spaces provided for the copy of the Report.

Signature of Seaman..

NOTE.—*Any person who forges or fraudulently alters any Certificate or Report, or copy of a Report, or who makes use of any Certificate or Report, or copy of a Report, which is forged or altered or does not belong to him, shall for each such offence be deemed guilty of a misdemeanour, and may be fined or imprisoned.*

N.B.—*Should this Certificate come into the possession of any person to whom it does not belong, it should be handed to the Superintendent of the nearest Mercantile Marine Office, or be transmitted to the Registrar-General of Shipping and Seamen, Tower Hill, London, E.*

A discharge certificate. Bideford is a small port town on the estuary of the River Torridge in North Devon, South-west England.

Poplar is an area of the East End of London, in the London Borough of Tower Hamlets.

EXTRACT FROM IMMIGRATION ACT OF FEBRUARY 5, 1917.

187

STATEMENT OF MASTER OF VESSEL REGARDING CHANGES IN CREW PRIOR TO DEPARTURE.

DEC 26 1922

U. S. DEPARTMENT OF LABOR
IMMIGRATION SERVICE

Port of New York
24 Dec 1922

I, master of the British s.s. Bradford City from port of Liverpool hereby certify that the following is a complete record of all changes in the personnel of the crew of said vessel since arrival at this port:

Total crew at time of arrival 39 — Number of seamen deserted one
Number of seamen discharged — — Seamen left in hospital (or dead) —
Number of seamen signed on at this port one — Total crew this date 39

Dec 8, 1922

The above-named vessel arrived at this port 8/12/22 1922, consigned to U.S. Navigation Co. Inc.; is now lying at Brooklyn and is expected to sail 24 Dec 1922, for Liverpool

First port of call in United States this voyage was New York

Following is a detailed and accurate statement of all changes in crew:

DESERTING SEAMEN.

Name.	Age.	Nationality.	When and where signed on.
(20) Hayam Saleh	25	Aden, British	Liverpool 14/11/22

When he finally arrived in the States, he quickly joined other Arabs in Brooklyn, New York. He also traveled back and forth to Lackawanna where he maintained strong ties to family and friends and held onto a laborer's position at the Bethlehem Steel Plant. Word of mouth traveled easily among the Arabs in America, particularly within a close geographic distance and Papa's network both brought him initially to and kept him informed about work opportunities in Lackawanna. With so much work in those days, even despite temporary layoffs, many Arabs simply settled in close proximity to the Plant to facilitate the commute to and from work. And with many of them working swing shifts around the clock, the area south of Buffalo became the logical choice.

Of all the Arabs living in the area, especially those working at Bethlehem Steel, it was most likely for the Yemenites to derive a sense of comfort from staying close to their own. Papa was actually on a leave of absence with Bethlehem when he decided to open up a boarding house with his cousin on State Street in Brooklyn. Mom says that it was more like a large apartment building. Considering the potential of the "hotel" business, his long-term plan was to leave his position at the Plant and make his living in New York. But Papa did not want to give up his work at Bethlehem, mostly because he actually made more money there than he did at the boarding house at the time.

Deliberate about his posture even in his fifties, Papa appeared tall, strong and lean, but he really was not very tall. At best he had been 5 foot 8 inches but was always rather slender, so never an imposing figure. He usually dressed in dark or earth tone colors, but generally well, in a sport coat with a couple layers of sweaters underneath and always a fedora. In fact, sometimes the number of clothing layers he wore under a sport coat caused him to look like a larger man. Since he often behaved like a man twice his size, that was probably a good thing.

Papa with Mom, in Lackawanna, around the time they married.

He called it "sport," as he donned the inexpensive version of what I assumed was a pejorative reference because of how he referred to people who needed to feel like "big shot" as those who *dressed sport*. Although he was not finicky or vain, he always kept his one pair of black dress shoes polished, usually with Vaseline and an old rag. He had dark skin and curly, wiry salt and pepper hair that grew long only from the middle of his head down and often managed to get tangled. His face was small and structured with deep set eyes and prominent ears and nose.

His given name is Haziam, pronounced with a silent "i," and while his surname is Saleh, he had another name. I don't really know how it is spelled but it sounds like El-Gahim. That final name would identify which Saleh you were but it doesn't mean anything outside the culture so Papa dropped it. Saleh can be spelled with an i, Salih, or an a, Salah (meaning social virtue, an ethical term in Islam), but it means 'the righteous,' 'virtuous,' and it is the name of one of the prophets in Islam. The practitioner of Salah is referred to in the Q'uran as a Salih (feminine, saliha), a morally upstanding individual who works for the betterment—*islah*—of himself and other Muslims. So I guess it's a good name.

We know that the first name of Papa's mother is Fatima or Fatma. It is the name of the prophet Mohamed's daughter. I believe that she was deceased at the time his father took a second wife, who apparently had her own children. This caused my father to get lost among numerous siblings, those newly born of this latest union and those originally a part of the family. Papa never spoke much of his father's new wife, insisting only that she did not like him. Possibly this is what hastened his early departure from Yemen, for he loved his country, spoke of it often in impassioned terms, but was gone by the time he was in his early twenties and as it turned out, never returned.

The ships had offered an easy way out for audacious exit seekers. Papa was young, strong and resourceful enough to get along on his own. He was easy to work with, being open to various assignments on board ships and capable of cajoling not just a few people in charge. He spoke often of engaging in activity that today I would call *fake it till you make it.*

Whaddaya gonna do? He often shrugged half-jokingly when questioned about this, indicating that one does what he has to do, trusting, of course, that it will ultimately get you where you need to go.

On the economic and social strata, Yemenites do not take a high position, not in the U.S. nor among other Arab groups. But most if not all of the Yemenites I know are a gentle friendly people, proud and industrious with a keen sense of duty and loyalty so they never forget families back home. If and when they came to America, it was the opportunity to make a good living while continuing to send money along to relatives in Yemen. Many send money to family for their entire lives, whether or not they themselves returned to the land. This was Papa's practice as well. With such strong family bonds and economic orientation, it is not unusual to find Yemenites living in a home with several generations under one roof. They are a religious and hospitable people, too, opening their home to visitors and feeling hurt by those who decline on offers to dine along with the family.

******

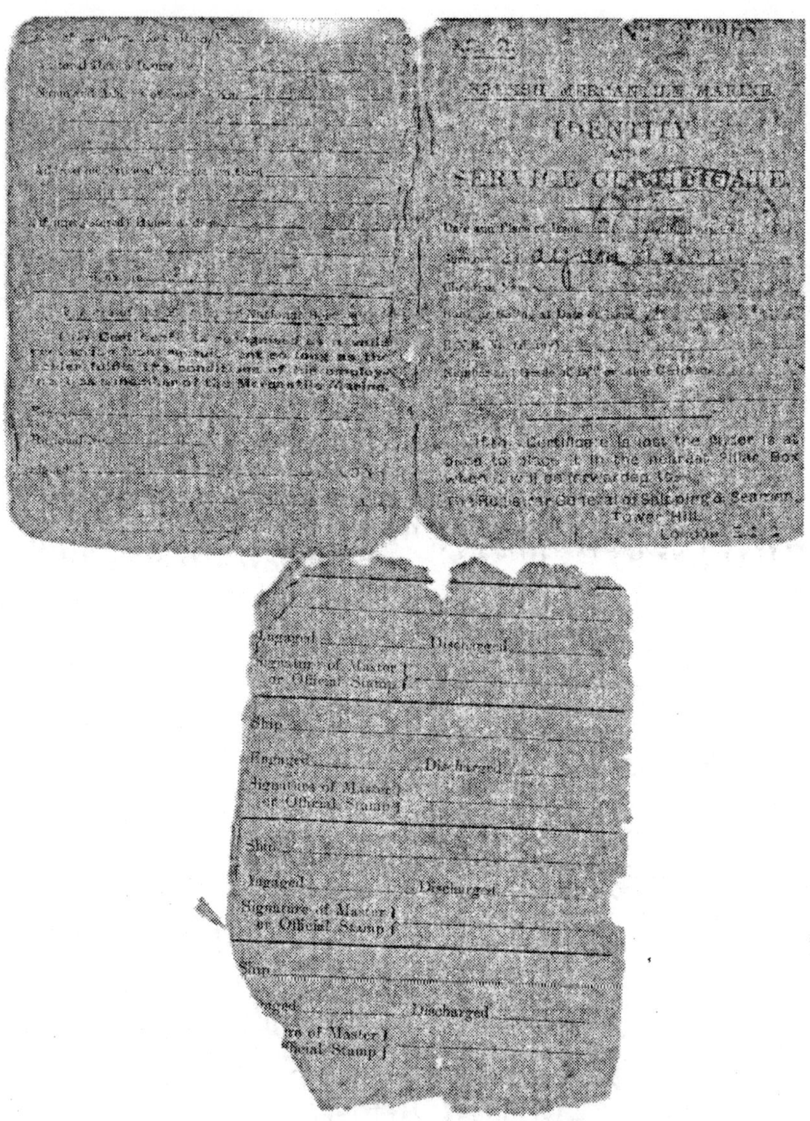

BRITISH MERCANTILE MARINE

IDENTITY

AND

SERVICE CERTIFICATE.

Date and Place of Issue

Finder of this Certificate is asked to place it in the nearest Pillar Box when it will be forwarded to

The Registrar General of Shipping & Seamen,

Tower Hill,

London

This Certificate is recognised as a valid ... so long as the holder fulfils the conditions of his employment as a member of the Mercantile Marine.

Engaged ... Discharged

Signature of Master or Official Stamp

Ship

Engaged ... Discharged

Signature of Master or Official Stamp

Ship

Engaged ... Discharged

Signature of Master or Official Stamp

Ship

Engaged ... Discharged

Signature of Master or Official Stamp

Papa's voyage out of Yemen began with the British Mercantile Marines.

972218 AZ UNITED STATES OF AMERICA
OFFICE OF PRICE ADMINISTRATION
WAR RATION BOOK TWO
IDENTIFICATION

OFFICE OF PRICE ADM.

972218

(Name of person to whom book is issued)

(Street number or rural route)

(City or post office) (State) (Age) (Sex)

ISSUED BY LOCAL BOARD No. (County) (State)

(Street address of local board) (City)

By (Signature of issuing officer)

SIGNATURE

WARNING

WPA Form 402 NOTICE OF CHANGE IN WORK STATUS

Employee's name ______ Identification No. ______

Address ______ Date ______, 193__

Certified from relief rolls ☒

Case No. ______ Relief dist. ______

Non-relief person ☐

Now working as ______ (Assigned occupation) Code ______ On project No. ______

Location of project ______ (Address) (City or village) (County)

Rejected ☐ Laid off ☐ Discharged ☐ Injured ☐ Resigned to take private employment ☐

Resigned because of illness ☐ Resigned for other reasons ☐ Resigned for reasons unknown ☐

EXPLANATION:

(Signature of foreman or supervisor)

6 RETURNED TO FOREMAN

Approved by ______ (Signature), Title ______

Effective date of change ______, 193__

U.S. GOVERNMENT PRINTING OFFICE

During layoffs from the plant, Papa could return to business with his cousin in Brooklyn.

U. S. MERCHANT MARINER'S DOCUMENT
UNITED STATES COAST GUARD

NAME: Haziem SALEH

Z OR BK NUMBER	DATE OF BIRTH
Z-754191	1/10/96

PLACE OF BIRTH	CITIZENSHIP
Arabia	USA

HOME ADDRESS: 170 State St., Brooklyn, N.Y.

PHOTO

SIGNATURE OF MARINER

He was obviously still involved on the seas with the American Coast Guard after he became a citizen.

DATE NATURALIZED	NATURALIZATION NO.	DATE FIRST PAPERS	ALIEN REGISTRATION
6/13/46	#6664759	—	—

HEIGHT	WEIGHT	COMPLEXION	COLOR HAIR	COLOR EYES	SOCIAL SECURITY NO.
5'6"	115	Dark	Black	Brown	134-01-0[illegible]

ENDORSED AT New York, N.Y. (PORT)
ON 4/10/47 (DATE) FOR
Wiper

FOR [illegible]

When the Suez Canal opened in 1869, it initially facilitated the migration of Yemenis like my father. There were difficult times and the west offered a way out of the already challenging fiscal and social development of the country. Yemen had been conquered by the British with Aden, a port city, becoming a protectorate way back in 1839. Ten years later, in 1849, the Ottoman Empire returned to extend their power over Yemen until finally retreating in 1919. But the Turks did not withdraw its protectorate area around the southern port of Aden until 1967. The British finally recognized Yemen's independence in 1925, just after Papa had decided to permanently leave on a ship that would eventually lead him to his new country.

The Ottoman era in Arab lands lasted until World War I when the Turks fought with the Germans and lost against the European allies of Britain and France. Arabs had actually provided the British with military assistance in exchange for a promise to help set up an autonomous Arab nation once the war was won. But when Britain and the other Allied forces (including France, Russia and the US) defeated Germany, it collapsed the Ottoman Empire. With France and Britain in the power position over much of the Arab region, they divided the fallen Ottoman Empire between them and in effect colonized most of the Middle East, reserving Palestine for a Jewish state. It was after this Great War that so many Arabs decided to come to the United States, the time when the seed was also planted for Papa's departure. He arrived in America just before limits were placed on immigration in 1924, with the Johnson Reed Immigration Act that ended the great exodus.

The steady migration of European Jews to what was then called Palestine continued in larger numbers following World War II. By this time, Papa was well established on American soil, but kept his ever-watchful eye on the events that involved the Arab people. In 1947, the UN voted to partition Palestine into Arab and Jewish states and in 1948, Israel was declared a Jewish state causing an exodus of hundreds of thousands of Arabs. Papa told us that this was how all the hostility began that continues to this day.

Papa also said that after the war in 1948 when Egypt & the Arabs lost to Israel, Aden was never the same again, perhaps discouraging him from ever returning, especially to live. Then, by the time of the Suez Canal crisis in 1956, Yemen's economy was on the verge of ruin. Papa had lived through so many pivotal historical events that he was only too happy to share and most of what I learned and what I thought about it came filtered through him and not through my school books. And although Papa had distinct opinions about the actions of his now two beloved countries, he never wavered in evenhanded assessment of each situation where both were involved.

Father and Mother

As a young Arab immigrant in America, Papa apparently enjoyed women and song. *Amrikan women, they luf me, yaa Dolah, what can I do?* He teased on more than one occasion. I never really wanted to know any of the details. I saw his picture as a young man, and I understood my father's attraction to women. I believed him, but like many daughters, I had no interest in having any information about my father's love life. So when he wanted to get into that particular mode of story telling, if my husband was around, he would grab him at the shoulder and whisper into his ear. The way Papa whispered, one got the sense that he really did not concern himself with how others in close proximity might hear him:

I can't help, yaa Jack. They luf me too much, the Amrikan women! Let me tell you eh—story…

And after a little snicker, they were off in some direction while Papa reveled in repeating one of his accounts on the abundant opportunities that somehow presented themselves, the ensuing frolic and irresistibility of it all.

Still, as much as he loved to think about women, to look at them and likely see a number of them socially, he would eventually settle on one, my mother. He met her while he was still part owner of the State Street boarding house in Brooklyn. Her mother had recently remarried and was temporarily renting one of the apartments in Papa's establishment with her new husband, Henry, until they could find a building to purchase. Mom rented one of the apartments too, and she and my father met. In her early twenties, she had been working full time after the war, making her way as an independent woman.

Although Papa was at least twenty, perhaps twenty-five years older than mom, they began to see each other and Papa told her of a place only four hundred miles away that was not so 'crazy' as the big city. He was still on a leave of absence from the plant at the time he met my mother but he was missing life in Lackawanna and brought that in to his daily conversations with her. He had ties there, he explained, a job too, and since Mom never really cared too much for the big and busy New York City, the quiet of Papa's smaller city sounded appealing.

She did well at work, always performing above expectation, but Mom rarely became attached to her job when she was still very young. If there was an area in which she demonstrated self-assurance it was in her work. She had quickly developed confidence in her ability and appeal to prospective employers with her hard work ethic and felt comfortable about future job prospects. With only a high school education, she applied for and easily obtained factory jobs. At the time she met Papa, she was taking the subway back and forth to work as a packer of Detector scales under the Brooklyn Bridge. To hear her describe the transit experience, she was "pushed" into the subway cars every day—not a pleasant memory for the demure young woman that she was.

Some time after my mother and father began dating, Mom had gone to work at a zipper factory, having answered an ad in the paper. It was more money, she told me, so off she went, performing so well that one day, some time after she had stopped coming in, her Jewish boss sent someone to her mother's home looking to offer her a promotion. In those days Mom said, there was no such thing as "giving notice" to leave your job; when you were done, you simply stopped coming in.

The woman at my grandmother's door was named Theresa. She was the "floor lady" who had recommended Mom for the job, reporting that she was the 'best worker,' one who was dependable and learned very quickly.

Is your daughter in? Theresa had asked, once she identified herself to my Grandmother.

No, she is gone out of town, my Grandmother had explained.

Oh... well, when will she be back? Asked the small, thin, dark-haired lady.

Oh, I don't think she will be back, said Grandma.

For some reason, Theresa had brought a photograph of herself when she came to call on my Grandmother.

I see. We miss her at work and we would like to offer her a permanent supervisor's position if she returns. Would you please give her this photograph?

After exchanging a few more pleasantries with the nice Italian lady, my Grandmother took the photograph and bid her farewell. And she did hand it over to my mother the next time she came to Brooklyn for a visit. Perhaps Theresa wanted to ensure her identity to my mom in case Grandma would forget. Maybe she just wanted mom to have the picture as a good-bye present. No matter. It was too late. The excellent employee and prospective supervisor had already left for Buffalo with Papa and would never again return to New York City to live.

Within a one-year period, my parents had decided that Papa would sell his interest in the Brooklyn apartment building with his cousin, allowing them to be off to Lackawanna to marry and begin a future together. Mom never said, but given their age difference she may have been seeking more of a father figure at the time. There was never anything too memorable about her biological dad and she was up for the chance to try something perhaps more stable with someone older and wiser in a town that promised to be more manageable. Papa had probably already made the decision to remain in America for his lifetime and this friendly, pretty woman with the big smile just made it easier.

The two people who would become my parents really did not have much of a courtship in New York. Papa was available and not such a young man and Mom wanted to take the next step in her adult life. When mom returned back to the apartment after a hard day's work at the factory, she wouldn't be going out on the town; she would stay in to rest for the next day, taking time now only to talk with this nice man she would forever call by his last name, Saleh. And on the job, between dealings with other guests and boarding house business, Papa was available to listen. Mom would speak of her discontent with the hectic life in New York and encourage him to tell her more about his "other life" upstate in Buffalo and Lackawanna. He easily entertained her with stories of what it was like there, including all the social activities he enjoyed and the places he loved like Niagara Falls and the nearby parks and beaches. People traveled by car and perhaps bus but there would be no subways in Buffalo. This was music to her ears. It seemed that whatever he had to say simply interested her. She was ready for a break in her work life, too, and recognized that this opportunity to join Papa and be taken care of just might mean that she would never need to work again. That *could be nice*. In any case, she was up for the adventure.

Mom had always felt like a stranger in New York, enthusiastically revealing her distaste for the fast life of the concrete city. Once she arrived in Lackawanna, she had an immediate recognition of the difference in life's pace there and appreciated even the tiniest conveniences that a smaller city would naturally offer. Mom felt happy and at home in her new city; it was all that Papa said it would be. Transportation was simple, traffic was entirely manageable and life all around was at a more comfortable pace.

They were temporarily at home in an apartment on Hamburg Turnpike—a street conveniently situated across from Bethlehem Steel. This is where Papa taught Mom the basics of growing her own vegetables.

I show you, Papa had said, and Mom listened.

He *knew* stuff. She is interested in learning, especially the things of the slower life.

Like this? She asked lots of questions and didn't mind getting her hands dirty, in fact, she was delighting in it! They had discovered a spot in the back yard of the building and began to grow vegetables like tomatoes, cucumbers and lettuce. Mom enjoyed this new experience and adopted a lifelong practice of gardening.

During the time that their first three children were born, they were a sociable couple, regularly going out to the cinemas, nightclubs and theatres. There were many parties, too, the ones that they attended at the homes of others and those that they frequently hosted. Visiting was a routine pastime with people seeming to take turns at "stopping by" each other's homes. These were occasions for lots of conversation and the sharing of a meal with an abundance of good food and *khubz* (bread), always the *khubz*. The easy, slower, family life.

In Lackawanna's robust Yemenite community, Mom took pleasure in the many Arabic festivities, haflis (dances), where she and Papa thoroughly enjoyed dancing the Arabic group dance, the *Debke,* and watching the performances of many entertaining belly dancers. She quickly and easily made friends. Papa was happy, too, he was finally settled down, getting lots of steady work at the Plant, and soon a child. When it was time to move out of the apartment on Hamburg Turnpike, where they shared space with other Yemenites in transition, they soon heard of a home for rent in Buffalo, nearby other Arabic families. It had two "flats," one upper and one lower. Papa would rent both floors from the lovely couple, Joe and Mary Corto, and sublet space to his cousin Mohamed in the upper flat.

Joe & Mary Corto were the ideal landlords. They loved Papa's consistently prompt payments and Papa loved that they were "good people." They would agree upon a payment schedule and Papa would personally deliver the money each month that would often result in a social visit. The Cortos and Papa became lifelong friends.

The downtown community of their new location in Buffalo was

very cozy and quite convenient. They furnished the entire home on credit with Zolte's, near the popular east side Broadway Market. The appliances were all from Sears. These rather substantial purchases marked the beginning of Papa's well established first rate credit rating, highlighted in folded booklets that hand-recorded beginning charges and steady payments and over-payments until it reached zero balances. Even after it had been stamped "Paid in Full," Papa kept those books for what seemed like prideful testimony of his reliability and integrity. But who knows because he rarely threw *anything* away.

One neighbor proved more friendly than most, knocking on the door one afternoon after my parents had moved in and were still settling in. She wasn't reserved like Mom; she was out there, assertive, insistent and to hear Papa describe her, could persuade sheep to become lions.

Hi, I'm Edith, she said.

I live just a few doors down. Let me know if there is anything I can do for you.

Within short order, and without mom saying much because she wouldn't—especially when it came to asking for help—Edith recognized that Mom could use a good deal of assistance. It was mom's first experience in putting an entire home together and Edith was a self-proclaimed pro.

Put this here, get this for that, let me show you how to put up these curtains.

Mom was eager to learn and receptive to advice, grateful to the seemingly savvy woman with whom she could easily talk. And since Edith seemed to know everyone in the neighborhood, she was able to introduce mom to many fine people who continued to remain friends for many many years. In later days, some of them were those she and Papa counted on to watch over us kids in the intervals when they were both at work.

Eventually Edith grew out of favor with Papa. He was vocal about his belief that she was instrumental in Mom's moving away from her marriage. After all, she was someone who began seeing another man and suddenly ended her marriage to a wonderful husband of whom my parents grew very fond. It was also well known that she had given her only daughter to her mother to raise. Soon after she re-married, the lovely first husband took his own life, shocking and causing enormous sadness for both my parents.

She's a "home wrecker," Papa warned mom, time and again.

I remembered this because not only had I been unsure of the meaning of the word at the time but I found it difficult to comprehend that *my father* could come up with such a term. I mean, I'm sure it was not often heard in common every-day English parlance. One day, many years later, Mom stopped speaking with Edith, saying only that once you befriended her, *she told you what to do; she owned you.*

Mom never collected people like Papa did. Once a person came into Papa's life, they were friends for the duration. Mom's life was consumed with working, transporting herself back and forth to jobs and finding time to attend in whatever way she could to five growing children with varying demands. It simply filled her days and most evenings leaving precious little time for friendships, although that may have been by design rather than chance. And mom was employed well into her 70s. Until I matured, I judged that about her. I thought that once she stopped working, it might be nice for her to have people with whom she could chat, lunch or shop, especially in her 80s, when it seems younger people are too busy and fewer are alive the older one gets. If she hadn't cultivated those friendships all along, it was sure there would be no one available when she finally had the time. I have considered how the experience with Edith may have left her with a so-called bad taste about that level of involvement.

Today I see a wife who was so unlike her much older husband in younger times now become vastly similar in day to day behavior. Mom's social life is limited to her five children and their children, most of whom live within thirty miles of her. Of her ten grandchildren, now almost three great-grandchildren, only two so far had relocated and returned for family. The ebbs and flows of her relationship with each of us has settled into a steady, mutually caring and for the most part, understanding one. Her acceptance is inspiring, wanting only for her children to be happy, like most moms. The support of one another, just as Papa taught us all, is good. For me, for sure, it is only second nature to always be there for anyone in the family and perhaps my siblings would say the same. Papa's many admonitions, especially for us to *stick together*, stay with me, those he spoke in English and those adages of his native culture, to which he often referred.

******

Our family was at home on the bottom floor with only two bedrooms and one bath. Two years after the first daughter came another little girl, and exactly two years to the day later, a boy, thank heaven, and finally two more girls, only sixteen months apart. Since he absolutely loved children, Papa was elated, and perhaps due to his years at this point, he could be a devoted father, only interested in providing for his large family. He had steady work, a nice home and a busy family life. It was better than he could imagine. But there was a problem. His wife, the mother of his five children, was not particularly happy.

It began somewhere around the arrival of the last two children. Mom felt restricted by her life at this point, as Papa had stringent rules for her and for all his children. There were growing differences and they were fighting about a lot of little things. When she began to spend what he considered an excessive amount of money, Papa threatened to remove mom's access to credit cards. The fight over money escalated whatever tensions already existed.

He took away all my charge plates, mom said,...*except one*. It was Sears.

The "Sears plate" was the one with which she would ultimately prove herself in order to establish credit in her own name. *Thank God for Sears* she'd said; it enabled her to obtain various credit cards for all the better clothing stores and other retail business establishments. Mom was also greatly assisted by one kind gentleman whom she would approach at Liberty Bank for personal loans to pay our catholic schooling.

He took a chance on me, trusted me, Mom said, and she would never let him down.

He granted her many loans after that first one, for a car and other purchases that would continue to liberate her. She never ever forgot the banker's kindness. She could not have done it without him.

Papa's interpretation of Mom's need to become financially independent was that she had been influenced by her "Amrikan friends" who did not care about hurting our family, our stability. He believed that they encouraged her autonomy and would inevitably re-ignite her desire to work and have her "own money." We don't know if that was true but what we do know is that *she liked it.*

Mom had had five children in only seven years, was only thirty-five years old with a husband near sixty years of age. She missed her independence and did not like all the rules and especially disliked the idea that someone would dictate how she should spend money. She knew she wanted all her children to attend Catholic school and anticipated a fight to get Papa to pay for it. She would regain her freedom with full time employment and pay for our schooling and the extras that she thought we should have. Having always been a hard worker, she took pride in and enjoyed the sense of accomplishment that she derived from having her own money but a full time working mother was not accepted practice in the Arab family structure. For Heaven's sakes, it was not yet particularly accepted practice for *American* moms to be working full time outside the home!

Moving Day

When there was no middle ground, no compromise to work toward, Mom decided to leave. She took a part time job right in the neighborhood inspecting washed vegetables and had decided to rent space from another Arabic man who lived a couple of blocks away from us. We had been without her for a short while at the time, but she had not yet officially moved out.

Then one Saturday, while we were all at home, Papa dressed in only a white undershirt and charcoal grey trousers, there was a knock at the door. When he went to answer, he saw two uniformed police officers and Mom standing behind them. The officer who spoke was kind but firm, instructing my resistant father to allow her to pass into the home to retrieve her "personal belongings." We kids heard the booming voices and all ran to my father's side. They went on to explain that she could take nothing else, as if that was supposed to have been some sort of consolation. That was the start of a day when there would be endless discussion and crying and noise that seemed unbearable. Papa would let her in, but not without a plea to the officers.

Look, he said, as he pointed to his children now standing along the wall, traumatized into silence:

How she leave five children? How you understand that?

I remember feeling as though Papa had won them over, as evidenced by their empathetic faces and nodding heads. But the officers were only there to do their jobs, to uphold the law.

Oddly, the one thing that kept the experience from being the most terrifying moment of my life was something Papa had said in response to a warning by one of the officers. As the policeman attempted to ensure that Papa understood the gravity of the potential circumstances of this matter, he intimated that the 'powers-that-be' would perceive such a situation—an immigrant male working swing shifts at the steel plant raising five children on his own—very negatively. *They* had the legal right to intercede. *They* could take the children away. But after Papa heard him out, he looked the officer right in the eye and said in a most convincing, straightforward manner:

They want my keet, they kill me first.

The forcefulness of Papa's impassioned declarative that day was his undying commitment that told me without question I would never have to worry about Papa ever allowing me and my sisters and brother to be separated from him. I never concerned myself about Father Baker's home again. I guess I must have also had to believe that *they* would never kill him, either.

At the time Mom moved out, my two youngest sisters were just babies. I am not sure how it got decided, but they would live with Mom for a few years until our father could handle all five children. That day could never have come too soon for Papa or my two little sisters, but in the meanwhile, they returned home from school with us each day, stayed until dinner time, and then returned to their house, about three blocks away. After dinner, while we played out in the street with the other neighborhood children, my sisters watched us through a back yard gate and an open field. I know how sad that was for my sisters and I can only imagine how Papa must have felt.

******

For Mom and my two little sisters, life was never tranquil living at 234 Carroll Street. Hidare, said to have originated from somewhere in Saudi Arabia, was incredibly strict and often demanding. They called him by his "home" name, but his real name was Ahmed Mohamed. When I think of him today, I sense that he was deep down a good man who had unfortunately experienced some great and unforgettable disappointment in his life up until we met him. I always felt an underlying sadness about him, even as a very young person. He had moments of sweetness and even times when he expressed a healthy sense of humor, but he was largely critical and often behaved in ways that were not such fond memories for any of us.

Once when Mom naively told Hidare that she had received a $.25 raise in pay, he raised her rent from $15 to $20 a week. In the end, once mom had gathered enough money together to go out on her own and decided to move out, he had given away several of her things before she could arrive with a truck to retrieve them. Mom had a beautiful phonograph that he did finally return to her but not before it was damaged. Hidare told her that the children next door to him must have broken it while they were there playing at his house.

It could not have been easy, but Papa somehow managed to become father and mother, strict and strong, yet sensitive and soft. He stayed with my sister Delilah all night in the hospital when she had her appendicitis attack and with my sister Minnie when she had to be hospitalized for four days for removal of a cyst on her hand. It was Papa who took two buses with me to have dental work performed under general anesthesia and it was he who rubbed my stomach to comfort me for hours when I was ill and had nightmares. In fact, whenever any one of us had a 'boo-boo,' it was he who proverbially kissed the spot and the hurt seemed to magically disappear. I mean, this was a man who blew bubbles on my abdomen and played *mutla* (the Arabic version of 'this little pig went to market…') on my fingers and toes to make me laugh. Papa expressed sorrow when a good friend passed away and was visibly shaken when his best buddy, our German Shepherd, Duke, had to be "put to sleep." There was nothing that any of my friends' mothers did that Papa would not or could not do. He cooked, washed clothes, cleaned—even if not very well—and shopped. We all benefited from his balance of protective manliness and sensitive 'motherly' nurturing.

The details of the separation placed obvious demands on all of us. After Mom left, there were wrinkled shirts and unmade beds, and too many pigtails in our hair. Papa's attempts to copy Mom's braiding resulted in disastrous styles that our schoolmates unfortunately did not miss the opportunity to mock. The very long and unruly hair of four female children presented the kind of undeniable challenge to a man already attempting to balance many life struggles. Shortening the hair was not an option and probably would only make the situation worse anyway. The numerous frustrations may have contributed to Papa's ultimate capitulation in allowing Mom daily visits to starch and iron our uniform shirts and place the respectable number of braids in our long, unruly hair.

I remember once when Delilah went up for Communion on a school morning, as we attended daily Mass before class for eight years of elementary school, and a few of the kids started jeering and pointing at her head. I just knew it was the multiple-braid ensemble that Papa had created for her, the best he could, and I felt really sorry for my sister. I squeezed my eyes closed hoping the moment would pass before I had to open them again.

Hair rituals were intense. In the beginning, we would sit on the floor between Papa's slender legs as he sat in a chair and gently attempted to first unsnarl our long curly hair with a brush and then create some type of decent hairdo. All the while we held on tightly with both hands clinging to our crowns, chins to chest to endure the agony. We knew he tried, but we could never be entirely satisfied. One day, when it was my youngest sister Sinia's turn, as Papa sat on the large burgundy velvet chair in the living room struggling to braid her hair, he confessed that it really was easier with boys because...*They no need ribbon and bow and what you call...?*

Barrettes, Papa.

Yeah, They no want fancy socks, too.

Soon all five of us had settled into a life with Papa, having our hair done by Mom whenever she could get there, in the mornings or even the night before on school days. As a matter of fact, her regular attention to Papa's missed details helped make life bearable. She had a new job now, a full time one, at Cadet Cleaners, accepting the night shift 6pm-2am, so that she could make more money and be available during the days when she felt we most needed her. She explained how to wash our white uniform blouses in a way that prevented them from turning yellow and taught us how to iron the shirts and even some tricks to managing our hair, especially once we refused to be satisfied with ringlets, a style mom insisted kept the hair contained and un-frizzed. Mom demonstrated much greater concern than Papa did for our appearance and how we were perceived by schoolmates or by those with whom we had daily contact and at the time, so did we.

As I look back today, I am entirely impressed with the amount of coordination and determination it took for my mother to step up to the plate in meeting the needs of her children, even as she did not live with us, even as she was financially challenged. It would always be her and not my father, who made certain that the five of us were at the dentist at least once each year, supplementing the payment for the visits, even as Papa's good health insurance covered a portion. It was she who would keep us updated and supplied with necessary school items and she who would often drive us to and from places for social events. It is the coordination, the scheduling, the insistence and dedication to ensuring that we were well cared for despite her absence, that is what impresses me today.

Nosey Neighbors

In the immediate aftermath of Mom leaving, there was a great deal of talk and scuttle about the issue of five children being left with only a father to raise them. A father who was gone often to work, different shifts at that. There were nosey neighbors and social workers and Children's Aid mildly threatening to either put us in foster care or a "home." Even at a young age, I was aware that any inference that these alternatives were somehow superior to a home with a loving parent seemed ludicrous. Still, for a time, even with my unquestioning trust in my father, it seemed close to becoming a reality. Had the law intervened, it is almost certain that things would have gone the other way. Foster care was unquestionably the most legally expedient. I know that we were scared for a while because it looked as though it was Papa against an entire big system—an American system—where he was undoubtedly ill-equipped and unfamiliar.

While fear was still the unfortunate reminder of our acknowledgment of this powerful and ominous "system," an incident occurred that I would never forget. One afternoon while Papa was still at work, I was on the street with chalk playing hopscotch all by myself. A lady walked slowly by, peering above her black spectacles with her eyes fixed on me the entire time. This was a lady we called 'the black widow' because she did not appear to have a husband and we never saw her dressed in anything but black. We often observed her sitting alone for hours on her porch watching passers by with never a nod or smile, always wearing a bland-colored kerchief over her head, double-knotted at the chin.

This time, the ever-watchful lady casually paused long enough to ask me where my father was. Her manner and tone immediately stirred suspicious thoughts in me, so I turned away and chose not to answer. She asked me if we all lived in the same house, and *how many of us were there, anyway*? Again, I did not answer. She asked me how my mother was. I declined a response once more and went right on with my solo game of hopscotch, keeping my eyes turned downward at the chalked street.

After she walked on past, I took my chalk and sketched a picture on the street of the black widow. I drew her scarf tied at the chin and gave her a long pointy nose, like a witch. I added a wart with pink chalk that Papa had brought home from the steel plant. Underneath the drawing, I penned my caption: *Mrs. Nosey-Body*.

Later on that same day, the lady took another walk and as usual, concerned herself with what was going on. As she approached on the sidewalk in front of our house, she turned her head to examine the street. I was sitting on the porch with my sister this time.

We watched as the black widow drew back with her one palm over her mouth. She turned quickly toward me and warned, *I'm telling your father, young lady!* Pointing at me with the index finger of her free hand. Then she posed an indignant stance and began to walk hurriedly back toward her home, several houses down from ours and across the street. I said nothing. At first, I got nervous. *What might this mean*, I finally asked my sister, once the lady was out of sight. *That wasn't a nice thing I did*...still, I did it; can't take it back.

When my father came home, I rushed to tell him the story. I didn't want her to get to him first. Remaining quiet while I explained, he listened to every word. I told him exactly what happened and how I felt about it all the way and I didn't stop until I was convinced I was thorough. And when I was finished, he asked simply, *That right*?

I think he was asking me if the way I described it had been accurate.

I responded. *Yes*.

Okay, he said. *When I see her, I tell her mind her own business and no bother my children.*

Besides being relieved, I actually felt proud; like I had behaved appropriately, as I had successfully followed Papa's instructions: *Tell no one anything. It's not their business.* I felt that my refusal to answer her intrusive questions was perhaps as ignorant as her asking them in the first place. But she did not deserve polite answers. Besides, my family kept to itself and we minded no one else's affairs; it was my opinion that it is a good and fair policy. Later, Papa spoke to me about the street drawing, letting me know that it was definitely *not necessary*.

With a strong family orientation and demand for self-respect, discretion was inevitably in order. Papa fiercely protected the family's honor and privacy at all times. As he was not always successful in securing an accommodating shift at work, his schedule might call for the day shift in the summer. This meant that the five of us were often on our own until he returned. Papa warned us to be careful of who we spoke to, of telling "our business" to anyone in light of the fact that there were those who simply did not have the best intentions. In light of the fact that there were ongoing, random investigations into *our case*. These were evidently the same folks who frowned upon five children being raised by a single working father. In those days, we knew that the local orphanage, Father Baker's, was too close and only too willing to take on children from "troubled homes." In the end, when it came to family ethos, discretion, protection and caution, we understood how we might be benefiting from lessons that Papa learned very much the hard way.

Papa wasn't really a suspicious type, but he did not have high expectations of others and had instructed his children well on the art of self-reliance. He had come to a new country when he was very young and had to figure out for himself the lay of the land and how to navigate his way around it. Probably a bit circumspect by nature in his more reserved manner, he had likely experienced disappointments along the way that reinforced a natural inclination. There was a practicality and earthiness about his thinking. He had conviction, was sure of himself and what he believed, perhaps coming to that in his later years, which is when he became a father.

Watch out for yourself and your sisters and brother, he must have said a million times.

Friendship can be fleeting, but family he said, *stick together*. His pragmatism allowed him to avoid disappointment and not be affected by others' opinions. His uncomplicated approach made it easier to mitigate the seriousness, as he laughed off and accepted so much more than many others did.

Papa's devotion to his family was unwavering, making our feelings his priority. He might have remained neutral about my "Mrs. Nosey Body" as he had no expectation of her, nor did he necessarily share our imagined fear of the harm she could cause. But because of his obvious sensitivity on the subject and concern for his children, he thought our personal business was not her affair and he found a no-nonsense way to tell her so. However it went, I got the feeling that she had not been offended and we never had trouble with her again. I always thought that if she had kept her distance, we would never know or feel either way about her and Papa could not have cared whether she was for us or against us. Her actions were an invasion of our privacy and forced us to care. Our family could only dig in our heels and remain united.

Of course, there were people who meant to be helpful and caring, and we had certainly found that to be the case. But this had been consistently diminished by the fair number of people putting in their two cents on what they felt should be done with our unique family arrangement. Some made judgments about it and had their opinions, the implications of which were threatening, especially to us children. There were intimations of interfering "authorities" who would use a reference book to determine the fates of five unsuspecting children. I thought *they* had no idea what it was like. They could not have known that we were all well loved and cared for and that we had not been neglected. They did not know and those who were most meddlesome did not seem to really care. They were nosey and their opinions were immaterial to me, my father, my sisters and brother.

Since Papa worked odd hours on swing shifts and often took advantage of regular overtime offers for the extra pay, it was necessary to employ baby-sitters. Unfortunately, they were not always nice. Each day, upon returning home from work, Papa would ask for and receive our play-by-play oral report of the baby-sitter's conduct and care of his children. That report would then constitute the basis upon which the baby-sitter was either retained or never again called.

One particular night, when Papa worked the late shift, 11pm to 7am, Delilah remembers because as Papa's oldest, she was appointed watchdog. He had given her a special phone number to reach him at the Plant and had arranged to have someone punch him out on the time clock if necessary.

You call me anytime, he had said, *If you need me, I come home.*

The two sisters who were watching us had slapped our brother, consumed just about everything in our refrigerator and ordered us all to bed. Now they were fat and happily spread out on the couches in the living room. This was the picture that finally moved Delilah to take advantage of the perfect opportunity to get Papa to come home. After hearing his watchful daughter's whispered report over the telephone, there was the reassurance:

Okay, Papa had told her. *Stay quiet now. I come home.*

In what seemed like a very brief time later, Delilah heard Papa come through the door and wake the two slovenly sitters.

Here, he said. *I pay you till today*, as he handed them their money and relieved them of their duties.

You no take care of my keet like I ask you, he added. *Go home, you finish here*! We never heard from the sisters again and it wasn't long after that when we convinced Papa that we were old enough to do without babysitters.

Love and Politics

66 Myrtle Avenue was a two-story red brick dwelling, but we would use it as a single family home, renting out only the upstairs kitchen and one bedroom. There was a gray chain-linked fence surrounding the mint garden to the left of the five painted concrete steps that led up to the front door, the red paint fading to reveal its original stone color, especially in the middle, the highly trafficked portion. The beige-paint on the front wood door was chipped in various spots and a window was cut in to the top half of the door that opened up into an entrance hallway. Immediately in front were stairs that took you directly to the upper apartment and to the left was another door that led you in to the downstairs flat where our family lived.

Papa told everyone that the mint in our garden had medicinal qualities. He used it in food preparation and in his tea, *shay*, along with ginger, but mostly he just enjoyed smelling it. *Here*, he'd pronounce, as he leaned over the fence, grabbing a chunk into his large rough hand and bringing it up to your nose, e-*smell it.* Then he'd walk away with the mint pressed up against his inhaling nostrils, pleasuring in its persistent aroma.

There was more than mint in the small square garden. Roses grew there, with prickly vines that climbed up the outside of the fence seeming to serve as a protector to the mint—not that there was universal appeal for the plant my father so coveted.

Two vertically rectangular shaped windows in the living room on the first floor overlooked the garden with a matching set of windows above them on the second floor. On one side of us was a single-family wood house where a quiet elderly couple lived until their house burned down. On the other side was an empty lot next to the concrete walkway that took you along the entire one side of the house and led you to our rickety wood-fenced back yard.

In the beginning, there were a number of Arabic singles and couples to temporarily occupy the upstairs flat. Most usually stayed only long enough to find permanent homes. Many Arabs lived with other Arabs while in "transition"…there were couples from Lebanon, Palestine, single men from Yemen waiting to get or go somewhere or another. For us children, it was fun getting to know all of them and sad each time they moved on.

"Azzizi" was the name we had for the old man who occupied the upper flat for the majority of our time there, but his real name was Mohamed El-something or other. We were told that he was a "countryman" who did not have any family in America so we needed to watch out for him. The elderly Arab kept rather quietly in his upstairs kitchen and one bedroom, so we were able to use the other rooms for extra space. And one might imagine that with five children and a parent living with only two bedrooms and 1 bathroom we needed space. Unfortunately, however, when Azzizi cooked, it usually involved eggs and onions mixed with some other interesting ingredient, which resulted in a fairly unattractive scent that permeated the entire flat for long periods of time. Papa was the only one that didn't seem to mind so it was usually he who would end up climbing the stairs at the end of the day to retire to bed.

Actually, Azzizi himself smelled like a cross between eggs with onions and boiled lamb. I think it was his clothing and how he washed them—if he even did wash them. He wore enormously thick glasses, moved slowly, and usually sat around smoking smelly cigars all day long while he awaited my father's return home from work to exchange some conversation in Arabic. A little hard of hearing and not fluent in English, it was frustrating for him to attempt conversation in other than his native tongue.

Sometimes Azzizi would leave in the morning and get lost for hours, shuffling along, cane in hand. No one ever knew where he went or how far he got because he walked so slowly. We knew nothing of whether he managed any communication while he was gone. We didn't know much of his background but there was something terribly lonely about him. I always thought Papa must have known Azzizi's story and that was enough for the both of them. They had a kind of agreement, spoken or not. Papa would be a true friend and Azzizi would report any nonsense around the house that he was able to witness while Papa was away at work.

Still, between not being able to see very well and having little tolerance for the busy-ness of five children, Azzizi was often crabby, discouraging any long-term contact with us. My brother Ed insisted on teasing the old man, causing Azzizi to get up from his chair and poke his cane repeatedly in the direction he figured was the source of his aggravation, all the while mumbling something in Arabic. I think it was a good thing for him as it got him up and moving, but Papa seemed very protective of his old friend and regularly warned my brother not to tease him. When the weather was good, we could see Azzizi sitting on the upper floor back porch with both hands resting on the top of his cane where he remained for hours at a time.

The portraits of Gamal Abdel Nasser and John F. Kennedy both hung on our living room wall as more evidence of Papa's split allegiance. These were cheesy prints in cheap frames and we were all a bit embarrassed by them, especially when we saw that the homes of our friends had well-framed paintings of landscapes and fruit arrangements and lovely family portraits or beautiful Victorian ladies on their walls. All we knew was that Nasser, an Egyptian, was considered a hero in the Arab world and JFK was a Democrat and Democrats were "the working man's" party, Papa's absolute party of choice. He once joyfully greeted John Kennedy, holding my sister up to shake Kennedy's hand when he campaigned for his election in

Buffalo's downtown Shelton Square. I think Minnie fell in love with politics that day.

The truth is that our home was really never very American looking after Mom was gone. It was strictly Papa's choice now, a hodgepodge of whatever, and mom never even commented about it.

My need to understand my father caused me to learn about the things for which he held strong emotions. So I investigated his two heroes. Gamal Abdel Nasser, born in 1917, was an Egyptian who grew up during the time of a "Brotherhood," one of the organizations whose purpose was to institute Islamic government in Egypt and free the country from persistent British domination. He came up from the military, having been involved in Egypt's 1952 Revolution that followed their defeat in the war of 1948 and emerged onto the world stage when he became president of Egypt in the mid-1950s. The Arabs revered him because he dared stand up to the Europeans. After having studied their influence on the Arab landscape, Nasser precipitated the Suez Crisis in 1956, which reclaimed the Suez Canal and appropriated revenues for the Egyptians. Although this audacious move nationalized the Arabs and made him their hero, there were questions about Nasser's dictatorial posturing as he took part in the already ignited fight against imperialism. Still, even as Nasser was responsible for helping end British rule, to this day I am uncertain as to whether Papa fully comprehended the impact of what was ultimately a non-democratic Egyptian government because he truly loved the democracy he lived in in America.

From Papa's perspective, Nasser and the revolutionaries desired to preserve Arabic customs, something he agreed had been threatened under colonial rule. He had considered that Nasser's socialist politics had credence perhaps due to his own early life exposure of meager means and an indomitable sense of fairness. He pointed to some Arabs in America who avoided Arabic names for their children as evidence of a subconscious belief in the inferiority of Middle Eastern customs. Papa was concerned about the process of "internalized colonialism" and thought that such distancing from native customs and the like demonstrated an unfortunate aspect of the European influence. And dismantling this influence was Nasser's critical contribution that keeps him in the hearts of many Middle Easterners as an important leader.

What-ew nation-hality?

Arabs were never nor will they ever be the only group that self-segregates. I have watched this tendency for a long time and it's just what people do, but back when Papa first came to the US and continuing until today, Arabs seem to consistently watch out for, take care of each other somehow. My greatest consciousness about this was not until later, of course, but there was and continues to be a definitive sense of community for most Yemenites like my father, and others, Palestinians or Lebanese with whom I grew up.

Papa teased about our Palestinian friends, saying they were really "Jewish" but then told us that the Jews were our 'cousins.' They were tough businessmen, Papa said, and proceeded to regularly conduct his furniture and jewelry business with Jewish storeowners, people with names like Maisel and Gamler and Zolte. All knew one another on a first name basis and I got the sense there was nothing but mutual respect and admiration between Papa and the businessmen. It was true that these people were either educated or welcomed into a world of the educated by virtue of their business owner status, whereas Papa, like so many other Yemenites, was a laborer and perhaps viewed in a different light. And although both groups came to the United States to make money, Papa's people generally succeeded due to hard work rather than a higher education.

The assimilation process may have therefore been easier for the Jewish folks who spoke superior English and lived among other Americans, usually in the better neighborhoods. The Yemenites were more clannish, wearing their national garb and living amongst other Arabs in more modest neighborhoods. One such area was located south of Buffalo, in Lackawanna, home of the Bethlehem Steel Plant where so many Arabs were employed. And while the Palestinian and some other Arab groups may have indeed been influenced by colonialization, naming their children European or American names, many Yemenis, like Papa, insisted on Arabic names. But those who demonstrated conformity for facilitated assimilation, Papa said, had *two faces*. They had moved toward their independence even while they secretly admired European institutions.

Relating numerous stories about his country, his culture and about having been an experienced shepherd on the top of the mountain, Papa really wanted his children to *be* Arabic, to *feel* Arabic. I can recall as a little girl sitting on his lap reciting and repeating the Arabic words for Mouth, *lakfish,* and point; nose, *nughratey*, and point; head, *ras*, point; leg, *wrigley*, point. *What nation-hality are you?* He'd ask with provocation. *American!* We responded, familiar with the game and egging him on.

What? What??? He insisted.

Arabic! We'd say.

Okay!!! He pronounced finally and emphatically as if he'd won another round.

Papa had threatened to take us to Arabia a few times in the early years when we were growing up, when it seemed life in America was sure to present insurmountable challenges to a single father with five children. The last time he mentioned it was about the time we were all around adolescent age or approaching it. The memory that I am left with now plays in slow motion: Papa about to mouth the familiar words, but when he begins, our eyes meet his and the words are rendered impractical and unreasonable. *How? How can we possibly uproot the five of us for a life of unfathomable difference*?

Papa was usually not an unreasonable man. He gave up on the idea of us living in Arabia almost the same way he gave up on his four daughters marrying Arabic men—a reluctant resignation born out of looking into the eyes of his five *American* children.

None of my siblings shared my enthusiasm for the prospect of relocation. I don't think they even thought Papa was entirely serious. But what I saw was the possibility of fluency in the language I loved and full-time exposure to his native culture. I spent hours contemplating this opportunity even as it held the fear of the unknown in a huge way. Exactly what I was going to do if life became oppressive, I don't know. I was just up for the adventure. I could cross that bridge if or when it appeared.

I never completely understood why we did not speak one hundred percent Arabic in our home, since Papa was determined for us to own our heritage. I know that immigrants who did not speak in their native tongue to their American born children were said to have been more concerned with fitting in and therefore encouraged English to be spoken even in the home, but Papa did not care about that. We all knew words for foods like *khubz*, bread, *lahma*, meat, *shay*, tea, *kahwa*, coffee, *batata,* potato and *khanzi*r, the bad pork word. And we, of course, learned many other Arabic words and expressions that Papa would continually bring into his English-challenged sentences, those that contained both languages.

We lived like Arabs and even like Muslims as we did not eat pork in our home, only kosher meats bought at a special supermarket named *Parkedge,* a special trip we took regularly to a northern suburb that happened to have a kosher department. But Papa even gave up on that eventually, once he realized we had been exposed to foods like hot dogs and ham, once we were older and had taken in a meal or two at a friend's home. The house rule then became cooking in separate pots, where Papa would never use the same pan we might have to cook any food that might contain even the slightest ingredient of *khanzir*.

A decent story teller, Papa regaled us with his 'old country' stories, living on farmland and herding sheep. Unfortunately, I hardly remember any of the details as I tuned out, especially when I recognized a repeater. I guess when you're a kid, interest level in things for which you lack association is limited to non-existent. But I do remember one story, perhaps because Papa told it so often.

His little brother's teeth had suddenly all fallen out at the same time. Apparently it was the opinion of their household that the little boy was the victim of an "evil eye" from a nearby village woman. The word for this reference is *hassad*, which began in the Islamic culture and passed on to the Arabic culture. It is mentioned in the Q'uran in several suras (chapters). It is meant to describe what occurs when a person is jealous and casts evil wishes on another and would not be satisfied until the other person looses whatever blessing (could be good looks, good teeth, etc.) he had. As Papa tells it, his mother instructed him to go up to the woman's cabin and to somehow get near the bottom part of her to cut off a piece of her garment. Papa said that he was successful and quickly brought the piece to his mom, who then burned the cloth and had his injured brother take in the aroma of the scorched remains. Soon after, Papa said, the little boy's teeth grew back and were...*perfect*.

Papa had traveled through many countries before finally arriving in the States to settle down. Living the majority of his life in America, he was grateful for the opportunities to earn money and live well. Nonetheless, he kept close to the social traditions of his country and had a lot to say about how the two cultures compared. Mostly, he favored Arabic customs. Still, his tolerance of, or better his obvious assimilation in to the American culture, almost at the expense of his own, had been a source of some confusion. I believe this to be the reason for my leaning toward the reality of our possible relocation to his country.

There were numerous times when he disparagingly referred to "the Amrikan system." When it came to things like what he perceived was promiscuous behavior and a lenient justice system, he had serious opinions. So one might think it even more antithetical to not insist on exclusive Arabic in the home and not demand that his children actively practice Islam. Although it was a definite suggestion, he never ordered any of his four girls to marry Arabs, even as he was never crazy about American boys. Papa had very strong leanings about the way he perceived American children, especially girls, were being raised, the permissiveness of the parents, etc., and he had often had great difficulty with how our country handled criminal offenses, citing recidivism rates as clear proof of its flaws. Still, he not only continued to make the U.S. his home, but he loved America for many reasons and wore his American citizenship with tremendous pride. He would never return to his original "home" that somehow I knew he missed so dearly. I felt he was forced to give up his attachment to many of his beliefs and cultural preferences in order to live here in peace, with his family, *in the Amirkan System* for the rest of his life.

It can not be that he never gave it much thought. Papa gave everything a great deal of thought. *I thinkin' too much,* he used to say, when someone caught him in one of his frequent pensive moments. He spent a good deal of time alone in his life, especially once all of us were grown and out of his home. I suspect much of that time was deep in thought about the past, present and future. Perhaps this is why I always felt that Papa had good reasons for all his decisions and I would be surprised if he had substantial regrets.

Although I continued to question his living in a place where he mildly maintained social disagreements, Papa's American system arguments made a lot of sense to me. Family honor and integrity are the cultural cornerstones of his people, making the notion of drawing unlimited weekly checks from the government unacceptable and difficult to comprehend. There is no pride or honor in taking "charity," as he often referred to our welfare system.

We could do a better job with our judicial system, too. *In my country*, he would say, *after two time you steal, they take one hand.*

And, in general, Papa thought Americans created the environment that encouraged, rather than discouraged, promiscuity. *She look bad*, was his comment upon seeing a young girl hanging out with boys, or *how her mother leave her like that*? He thought American girls wore revealing clothes and moved in seductive ways. His comic renaming of one neighborhood gal, referring to her as "Twist," was due to the alluring way she walked, which Papa felt her parents should have corrected.

But Papa's frame of reference on that subject was social segregation of the sexes with men physically distancing themselves from women. Personal contact is reserved exclusively for husband and wife and public displays of affection definitely discouraged. We could be outdoors in the evening only while Papa sat on the front porch watching. As his daughters, we wore slacks with zippers on the side, not the front (apparently a sex-related concern), and were never permitted to remain in the company of male visitors, particularly unchaperoned. While some of these rules seemed strident at the time, I came to see how the end justified the means, at least according to his culture. I understand how many of these views were almost like the Islamic tradition—black and white—easy to understand somehow. But then again, perhaps because I always felt caught between two culturally diverse worlds, I actually found myself acknowledging the merit in both points of view.

There is little doubt that the opposite sex matter did appear to be an obsession with Papa and most Arabs I knew. He once had me actually considering, even believing, that a kiss from a boy might result in my becoming pregnant. *That (is) trouble*, Papa would say, about groups of boys and girls permitted to socialize, inferring that this innocuous practice is tantamount to overt sexual temptation.

Arabic men kiss one another on both cheeks, but male-to-female greetings are conducted with nothing more than a handshake. Eye-to-eye contact between the sexes is vehemently discouraged, but it is customary—even insulting not to make eye contact-with a member of the same sex. Even inside the mosque, males worship separate from females.

I remember when I found out that according to the Q'uran a man may take up to four wives, which seemed to me a grand violation of the husband-wife fidelity bond, Papa defended it by saying that there are logistics involved. Often, if one woman can not bear the man a son, which is nearly considered a hardship for the man, he takes on another, usually younger wife to oblige this "right" of man. And, Papa said, as long as a man can afford it and the wives agree, it is acceptable, but not here,

No in the Union Estates, he'd said assuredly. *Only in my country.*

Along with daily efforts to encourage our Arab ness, there were the constants in our lives and Papa would never deviate from those. Each morning, as he awoke us for the school day, he appeared at the entrance of our rooms with the greeting of *Saba-el-khair*. At night before bedtime, we exchanged good nights, *Masa-el-khair*. Before we ate, Papa uttered the words of thanks to God, *Bis-mil-lah, El-hum-du-la-la*. When there was some anticipation, it was *insh-allah*, always a thousand times *inshallah*—submission to the will of God or *if God wills* (it). "*Il-la*" was the warning that consistently accompanied the name of the individual to whom the warning was directed. For me, this was the question, *why*?

He yelled at us in Arabic too, which was often quite funny, and he used Arabic commands like *Yala*, which was to come on, *Im-shee*, let's go or walk, and *khuba*, to cover, his oft heard command to his daughters whenever we would wear something just a bit questionable or sit in a certain suggestive manner—which simply never happened with the most modest four women I know but these were *his thoughts*. Of course, Papa taught us the numerous names for food dishes and numbers and alphabet. And he also used Arabic for affectionate terms directed at his children, which are unforgettably sweet memories.

I listened intently whenever he spoke Arabic to friends during home visits or while he spoke on the phone. He liked that I loved the language. I even memorized the lyrics of a few Arabic tunes and regaled him when I wanted to see him smile that contented way. Papa took great pleasure in any of my efforts to speak his language, but particularly derived a great deal of satisfaction when I sang these songs.

Yala, yaa Dolah, he would call out to me. *Sing 'Yaa Sitt*!'

And I would sing. And he would smile.

Sing '*Ish-ta-tel-ak*." It was not the title for the song but he knew that I understood which one I was to sing. This was an upbeat song. Papa listened while I crooned away, an entire song that I still hold in my memory. Sometimes his eyes were closed and his lips were smiling with contentment. Sometimes other people were present and he would ask me to show off my ability to them. I always complied, although often reluctantly, because I loved how happy that made him.

Looking for Mom in the Snow

I once read that earliest memories are supposed to tell us, at least in some measure, the story of who we are. In my case, it also reveals my parents. Late one night in the dead of winter, my sister Delilah, firstborn and two years older than I, stood in front of me at my crib. She had pulled down the railing and was carrying me to the floor. The next thing I remember is leaving the house completely dressed in snowsuit, boots and mittens. My five year old sister and I walked hand-in-hand down Myrtle Avenue toward Chicago Street in knee-deep snow, which meant that we essentially used our barely mobile little bodies as snow removal devices. We had walked about three-quarters of one block before we got to the corner of our street. Firemen caught sight of us from the window of the red brick Fire Station, which sat on one of the four corners. A man ran out and brought us into the station. He removed our gloves and told us to rub our hands up above the space heater. He said that he would find our mother.

Eventually the firemen found Mom having coffee at a friend's home across the street from where we lived. She apparently had placed herself purposefully in a position to look down at our front porch from an upstairs window where she had been sitting. Unfortunately, she still managed to miss our exit. Mom loved to visit with the women from the block and sometimes in late evenings, the women would take turns routinely stopping at each other's houses for coffee and conversation.

Talking with my sister many years later, she explained that she had awakened from a dream in which we were left alone. We figured our ages to be approximately two or three and four or five years old. As we spoke of the incident, my sister could recall her sense of urgency upon awakening that night. We were alone; she was afraid. We are sure that she had vocalized our dilemma as she dressed me in full snow attire. She was always explaining things to me, but that is verbal detail I could not recall due to my young age. We wondered together in our adult years about the prophetic nature of this "dream."

Mom was trusting and adventurous. Her explanation was that *it was safe back then*, a time when you would easily leave your children at home with the door unlocked late at night and simply go across the street for a visit with a friend. But as babies, we could not know what era it was, nor could my sister understand the difference between a brief step away and complete abandonment. Mom's independence, and perhaps naiveté, precluded that kind of empathy for the moment.

Papa was from a different school. In his book, there was no room for adventure or chance taking, especially with child rearing. With consistent hyper-vigilance, he would lie on the couch in daylight hours while we noisily played nearby, to catch a nap before a late shift at the steel plant. He was fine and appeared to be resting, even sleeping, as long as he could 'hear us.' But almost with mystifying precision, he would awaken the minute the room fell silent. We could never quite figure out how he managed to remain so aware and insistent in his slumber.

Drama in the Courtroom and the Search for a New School

Mom never fought Papa for custody and she evidently shied away from conflict, though I would hardly know that from the fights she and Papa would have before she left. Still, by nature, Mom was reserved and publicly reticent. She would definitely pick her battles, however. When she needed to become forceful and even combative, she rose to the occasion like one would not think possible. And there were two occasions in particular in which Mom demonstrated that she had what it took to standup for herself and what she believed in.

The first of these had to do with her insistence that we children be raised Catholic rather than Moslem. The actual court room drama had been preceded by a number of arguments between my parents. I don't believe that Papa ever liked us getting baptized, but when Mom had her first two daughters brought to the church to receive the first sacrament, Papa was only quietly reluctant. When his boy arrived, it was another story but Mom went ahead and scheduled it anyway. Perhaps Papa in the back of his mind felt that he could change things at a later date. And by the time the last two daughters entered into the family picture, Papa would become more vocal. This may have been exacerbated by the deterioration in their relationship by that time, but the fights were ongoing and difficult. Mom's determination would once again cause her to take the kind of action usually reserved for more assertive types.

She sought counsel. Obtaining the name of someone who could help from one who knew, she ended up taking Papa to court. When they met inside the courtroom, the judge asked mom to state her case and with her lawyer at her side, she told the judge that she did not want her children to be Muslim. She was a Roman Catholic and wanted her children to be the same. After a few moments, the elderly judge called for my father to step up to the bench.

Mr. Saleh, he addressed him, in a very clear voice.

Listen, sir, in this country, the children take the religion of the mother not the father. That is my ruling.

And that was it, Mom said. Papa never fought her about it again. Mom thought that he might have understood that he risked being jailed if he failed to drop the subject but I think he just was a law abiding citizen and as such would respect the court's ruling despite his personal feelings. He was living in America and if that is the law, he had to accept it. Papa took his laws and his rights (like the one to vote once he became a US citizen) very seriously. The other fact is that most Arabs respect religion in general and one's right to choose how to worship, as long as he believes in God.

The second time we saw mom's assertiveness come in to play was once she had made the decision to move her two youngest daughters out of St. Columba School. By the late 1960s, with the neighborhood in its steady decline and the kids from the nearby public school becoming more and more aggressive against the catholic school children, Mom's deepening concern led to a crusade to relocate my two sisters.

First she went to the eastside Polish area and approached the pastor of the largest parish there. *No*, he had said to mom, *they weren't Polish* and therefore were *not eligible to attend school here*. Then she went to South Buffalo and inquired about them being admitted to St. Theresa's. Mom was refused again on the basis of not being a resident of the community. They took only children from the parish, the neighborhood, mainly children of Irish decent.

Becoming frustrated and desperate but still determined, Mom headed over to Catholic Charities to get what she felt might be diocesan-wide answers. She explained her plight but the woman she initially spoke to did not appear to be moved.

Let me see what I can do, she had told my mother, and walked away into another room. After some minutes, she returned.

I am going to have you try over at the Cathedral School. I'll talk to them first and then call you at work and let you know if and when you can go there. See if they'll take them there. But no promises. It's up to the pastor at the parish.

And last thing she says to mom, *I wish you luck!*

Mom didn't know what she was going to do next if she was rejected this time. The next day, she took off a half day from work, went to her appointment at Cathedral School. When she arrived, she stood all alone in a room and prayed. When the older priest walked in, he shook her hand and mom thanked him for speaking with her. Then she cordially pleaded her case all over again—about the rough neighborhood and the public school children, the Polish parish, the one in South Buffalo and the final warning from Catholic Charities. The kindly priest asked what my sisters' names were and asked a couple of other questions. Then he told Mom that the decision was up to the Principal of the school.

If she takes them, he had said, *it's okay with me*.

When the principal, a nun, arrived, Mom noticed that she resembled someone she knew. Realizing that it was her wonderful supervisor, *the skinny Italian lady, Theresa, from New York City*, she made some small talk about that and they seemed to get on to a good start. The nun told mom that my younger sisters would be accepted on the condition that they keep up with their classes and mom assured her that they would. Later, she threatened her daughters for fear they may not understand the seriousness of this condition and the consequences of failing to meet it. Of course, with fear as the great motivator, everyone met the standards and expectations and got exactly what they wanted in the end. Mom made an extra effort to attend their school functions, trying as she did to fit in with the upscale professional parents and my sisters complied and achieved to result in successful retention and ultimate graduation.

Biding Her Time

Perhaps in stark contrast to my straightforward father, I considered my mom more complicated, more difficult to understand, so I didn't make the same effort to try as I did with Papa. But some things were easy to see, like her friendliness and kindness toward others. Her generosity, for as little as she had. Most people describe her, even today, as a very sweet and particularly positive person. She worked hard for everything she ever had, particularly for her children, getting them what she thought they needed, at the very least because other kids had those things. And even though she never had a lot, she never wanted anything that wasn't hers. In fact, even when it was hers and someone else wanted it, she readily gave it to them with no attachment or expectation. *It's how you give a gift,* she says. She has been a wonderful role model to me that way. So when she noticed one day during a visit to another Arabic lady friend that the lady had some of her cups and saucers that Hidare had apparently given her—things that were not his to give—the woman explained in her own defense:

You weren't there so he gave them to me.

The woman who wanted for nothing, as some said, half-heartedly offered Mom her things but Mom would not accept them, saying many years later when she related the story to me,

I thought…please take them!

It was Mom's way of saying that if the woman could take things knowing that they belonged to someone else, she needed to just keep them.

My two younger sisters ended up leaving Hidare's house before mom did. One day they just packed their stuff and never returned. Living with us was inevitable anyway, they just decided to choose the date, along with Papa's approval and encouragement. It did not take long for mom to finally get her own place, though. And the details of that experience simply demonstrated more about mom's character.

With affordability the major concern, Mom took a one bedroom apartment on a second floor in a South Buffalo neighborhood, renting from a woman who lived on the floor below. Doris, the "landlady," was slightly overweight and generally friendly but in a serious kind of way. She also had strict rules for her building tenants and she enforced them with a willful eye. One of her criteria for renters: No children. Mom decided that she would lie and how she even imagined getting away with lying about having five children I can not imagine and I do not think she even considered the reality or the consequences if Doris were to find out. She was simply desperate and needed to get settled somewhere once she left Carroll Street.

Since the one bedroom was an enormous room that accommodated twin beds with a great deal of space left over for two dressers, all furniture borrowed from dear old Doris, a couple of us stayed with mom regularly and periodically there were at least three of us, but it did seem to work out. We just had to be sure not to call out to "Mom" whenever Doris was around.

Since the rent included electricity, all lights were to be out by a "decent" hour. When a couple of us stayed up late and Doris mysteriously 'knew' of that, she warned my mom, assuming that remaining up until late hours meant that electricity was being used. She frowned upon any noise, coming in late, as she would always know because the warning bark of her dog announced us and we had to pass her door before ascending the stairs to Mom's apartment. We were to use the washer and dryer only during the designated time slots that were assigned to the apartment number.

During the day, the apartment was empty with Mom working full time and us kids still in school and work. One day, after mom became friendly with the lady across the hall, she quietly revealed that the landlady "visited" mom's apartment regularly during the day and even spoke of what mom had in drawers and things around the apartment.

There wasn't much to be done about that, Mom thought. After all, she owned the building, had keys to everyone's apartment. Besides, there was nothing touched, as far as she could tell, nothing taken. Wasn't much to take.

When Mom finally retrieved her belongings from Hidare's house, she returned Doris' furniture and ended up with an extra chest, an antique, which she placed in the apartment basement. But soon the landlady would complain about the chest taking up valuable space and mom's response was ultimately, *would you like it?* Doris accepted the offer and ended the complaints instantly.

One day, while still renting from Doris, mom's doorbell rang and she answered it only to find a gentleman standing there who asked her what she had been paying in rent. Mom responded quickly, thinking nothing of it at all.

Eighty dollars. She told the man. *Why*?

Mom had been paying that same amount for the entire period she'd lived there, which by now was around seven years.

Oh no! Remarked the suited gentleman. *You are supposed to be paying only sixty dollars. This apartment is under rent control.*

Mom told the man that she never heard of such a thing and that *It's okay.*

She was *fine*, she assured him. The man went on his way and apparently paid a necessary visit to the landlady.

Later that day, Doris came up to see mom. She was not angry as Mom had anticipated but rather asked my mom to do her a favor. Mom was to agree to tell anyone who asks in the future that she paid the lower rent amount.

No problem was mom's reassuring answer, even as she recognized what was happening. She never wanted to *cause any trouble.*

It was certain that mom's interest was to stay where she was. For now, she did not wish to uproot herself. Not yet. Not until she would finally have the money to buy her first home on her own. That would come about two years later.

Mom had received a small inheritance when her stepfather Henry passed away, which she quickly decided to use for the purchase of her first home. It was late fall 1977 by the time she found it, the year of the great Buffalo blizzard and the upcoming winter was stacking up to be almost as bad. Mom had settled on south Buffalo because of its affordability and her familiarity with the area, but the house, built back in the 1920s, needed a lot of work. The furnace failed and mom and I spent that first night huddled on the living room floor. After we survived that, we met a few gracious neighbors who were helpful, offering to keep us until the furnace was fixed so we didn't freeze to death. But mom was preoccupied with being less than happy with her decision. Back in those days and particularly given the naiveté of my mom with such a major acquisition, house inspections conducted as prerequisite to purchase were either non-existent or of inferior quality. It did seem a daunting adventure in those early days. Still, her trusty enthusiasm to make this home everything she wanted it to be would win out. Many years later, after I had greater awareness, I marveled again at mom and her companion, Stanley's courage and optimism in light of the obvious facts.

Security Issues

Like most families, we had fallen into certain rituals, once it was down to the six of us on Myrtle Ave. One of my fondest memories is what would happen nearly every time Papa was returning home from work during the day. We especially liked his 7 to 3 shift on weekends because we needed no babysitter and he was home for dinner. He would come generally from the same direction, having been dropped off at the corner of Myrtle and Michigan Streets, where he still had an entire block to walk. While playing in the street, one of us would catch sight of him and call out. We knew the form, could see the slender figure with the hat, *always a hat*, empty lunch box in one hand slightly swinging at his side and his unmistakable upright posture. We would immediately challenge each other to a race to see who could get to him first. Papa was in on the game and would cheer us on all the way.

He was always so happy to see us, my sister Delilah remembered.

But then, we were always so happy to see him, too.

Once everyone piled on, jumping up to kiss his cheek nearly knocking him over, his arms opened wide, enveloping the bunch of us while we panted and laughed all the way to our front porch.

It was Papa's love of games and contests that led him to constantly engage us in silly little tests of one skill or another. At amusement parks like Crystal Beach and Glen Park, after getting us something to eat and doling out dozens of ride tickets, he would plant himself at one of the game machines and set us free. We always knew where to find him because he either would not have moved, or not moved very far. Papa got such pleasure out of winning the little prizes playing Skee Ball and such games; it didn't matter how much he might have invested to be able to finally take home a token award, like ceramic banks shaped like animals. He would save them like trophies and pull them out to show visitors from time to time. There were some that actually got used but often they never made it out of the drawer that he first placed them in to "save" them. We would find the funny banks years later and laugh about it all over again.

******

Like my sisters and brother, I loved being with my father, but somehow I acquired the freedom needs of my mother, which drove both of my parents a little crazy. I can recall when I was very little often hanging onto one of his legs while he patiently kept still, resting a reassuring hand on my head. When he was not there, it seemed that all I could do is repeatedly ask for him and await his return. I think each of us associated a particular sense of security with Papa's mere presence; there was a distinguishing and corresponding feeling of insecurity with his absence.

Once, when I was probably not yet five years of age, I became frantic after a brief discussion with mother regarding the whereabouts of my father. I asked her multiple times—*Where is Papa?*

She had been cooking at the stove with her back toward me, motioning me to back off with her one hand and warning me to *stay put* as my father would soon return from the second floor. But in my five-year-old mind, any amount of time was too long to wait and after proceeding up the stairs for a cursory look, I decided that he was not there. Turning quickly on my heels, I immediately took it upon myself to embark on a mission in pursuit of my father.

The problem was, of course, that I had no plan. I simply set out like an undirected missile fully aware of my objective, but too immature to realize the potential magnitude of my search. I suppose I must have figured that somehow if I just kept walking, I would eventually bump into him. Besides, I was determined and obstinate, just had to find him. I had gone at least four good size blocks before a police car drove up.

Hello, little girl, and where might you be going?

Said the nice man on the passenger side, who also complimented my pretty red velvet dress with the big bow in back.

I promptly explained that I had to find my father, and then he asked my name.

I proudly responded in rote fashion: *My name is Dolah Saleh. I live at 66 Myrtle Avenue, Buffalo 4, New York.*

Recital of your identification information is one of those things positively reinforced when you are a child.

Well, young lady, why don't you hop right in and I will take you to your father, the nice policemen said, motioning toward his lap. Without hesitation, I climbed right up onto the friendly officer, thrilled that he would take me to my Papa.

It was fortunate for me that those two gentlemen in uniforms were, indeed, men of the law. I was so delighted with the news that my search was over, I neglected to heed the oft-heard warning about "talking to strangers," much less getting into a car with them.

As we reached our destination, which was of course, my home, I could see both my parents anxiously awaiting our arrival and was instantly able to determine which one was most delighted to see me.

Leave her down right there, officer. I'll take care of her, I heard my mother say as she gave me a stern look to let me know that I was in deep trouble. My response was instantaneous. I completely disregarded Mom's presence and ran into the awaiting arms of my happy-to-see-me father.

On another occasion, my friend and I had been busy at work digging the ground in search of worms to sell the neighborhood fishermen—an attempt at independence with our own "spending money." Jackie Taylor and I took turns holding up heavy rocks while the other would dig and place the fish bait into a jar. After Jackie had held up one enormous rock with both her hands for a time, she let out an emergent warning:

Watch out... I'm... dropping... it!

There wasn't time for me to extract my right hand. Wham! the boulder came down with full force, causing me to nearly faint and let out a scream that attracted not just a few people. I guess Jackie panicked because she took off running and yelled for help.

By the time someone arrived to lift my inanimate tormentor, I was frenzied with pain. The moment the rock was lifted, I guided my hurt hand atop my good one and held it tightly. As I did that, I caught a glimpse of the crushed middle finger. The blood and visible veins of that injured finger almost scared me painless.

Still in shock, I began to run. Running was always my reaction to hysteria and this time—pain. *No standing still for me, need to move or I will explode*! I ran around the block first with no thought at all and then, *what now*? I usually ran to my father when I was hurt in any way but Papa was unavailable. He was at work.

I circled our entire block three times holding my throbbing hand before someone stopped me. One of the neighbors put me in a car and took me to the Emergency Hospital's emergency room, several blocks away. I went reluctantly out of fear, but I would not allow the medical people to treat me until my father arrived. I knew he would be there as *soon as he got word*. Once I saw him, I could relax. He wasn't going to allow anyone or anything to harm me.

Feelings of insecurity in Papa's absence would continue to surface in each of us on various occasions. But it was not often that we were without him. In fact, I do not believe that he even had a personal life outside of work and his five children. I think we *were* his life.

Still, the desire for an intact family would never leave us, even with Papa's dutiful attempts to fill the shoes of both parents. And perhaps being a product of a culturally unique one-parent home had its benefits. It is true that in our youth, we were insulated and isolated from the outside world. We had rules, and never lost sight of who was boss. This was our frame of reference and as children we did believe that on some level everyone else lived as we did. By the time we all figured out that was not the case, we were the people we were going to be.

It is entirely possible that we spent more time not appreciating our unique situation. My brother missed having the all-American father to play ball with, and I was distressed over not getting to do things I thought every healthy American girl did in those days. Delilah sought a substitute mother and as the youngest, Sinia felt confused and lost much of the time. And there were numerous occasions for all of us that were terribly uncomfortable about not having an available, "traditional" mother.

Even with my minor complaints back then, however, I found a way to count our blessings. Probably inheriting the optimistic gene from my mother, I usually looked at the good side of circumstances. Even as a child I saw that Papa stepped up to the plate in a fashion that in many ways made Mom's absence less hurtful. He was never drunk, abusive or emotionally unavailable. I had been aware of minor examples of all those things in other families. Other than when at work, he was physically available as well, as when he would arrange to get home in short order when we needed him. He was my friend, our friend, and when he had to be, which was most often, Papa was our disciplinarian. Our memories are filled with times when he listened, how he showed he cared even if and when he disapproved of something we did. The disapproval was obvious, but he never attacked *us,* did not say mean, hurtful things that destroyed how we felt about ourselves. *Il la, yaa Dolah*, or whichever child he was admonishing, would signal a warning of objectionable behavior, which was usually adequate to nip it in the bud. The discipline was directed at what we *did*. That was very clear and that was all. You could leave the situation and start over, with more desirable behavior and your self-esteem in tact, knowing that you were still loved and cared for. He accepted us and loved us even when we probably did not deserve his love. In an almost artful manner, Papa had a way of trivializing without discounting our feelings. *That's nothing, yaa Dolah,* he would say as he pointed out the big picture that helped me place things in proper perspective. He called things as he saw them, even when it came to our mother, calling her behavior unacceptable but expecting us to love her anyway.

Sometimes, in an effort to avoid being disciplined, funny things happened and we are left with hysterical memories of being between states of scared to death and laughing so hard we were in danger of losing bladder control.

There were not to be any boys at all in our home. If they were the sons of what we considered family friends, they could be invited but only when Papa was present. One day, after Delilah had promised her friend Willy that she had an extra book bag that he could have, she said that he could come over to get it.

Hurry, Delilah told Willy after school, *if you come over, you will need to hurry before my father gets home from work.*

When Willy arrived, Delilah quickly showed him the high shelf on the left side at the top of the staircase leading down to the basement. He would need to reach up for the shelf in order to retrieve the bag.

No problem said Willy, who was taller than Delilah at the time, but he began to reach over just as Delilah heard the front door.

Oh my God, It's my father! She whispered frantically. *You've gotta get out of here*! Willy's position at that moment was midstream stretching to reach for the bag but in reaction to Delilah's escalating warning, he somehow lost his balance and fell all the way down the stairs—bag in tow. Delilah, who is at this moment stuck between panic and laughter, still manages to get the words out:

Hurry! Hurry! You've got to leave! Now, Willy! He'll kill me for Heaven's sake!!!

The mildly wounded Willy rose to a standing position, gathered himself and the coveted bag and ran up the stairs for a quick exit out the back door, still in stitches. Delilah still laughs telling this crazily innocent story.

******

There were not many people that Papa actually disliked, but when Mom left, he continually referred to that "American" friend who he believed somehow caused or at least encouraged the breakup. His pejorative references to her were disturbing to me since I felt so helpless and could also sense his helpless frustration in the matter. All I knew is that Mom chose her to be my godmother and she was somehow responsible for a highly regarded gentleman's death. Papa held Edith accountable, too, for our Mother baptizing us Catholics instead of allowing him to have us practice the Islamic faith.

But this was Papa calling an elephant an elephant. He made regular assessments of people's character, citing certain actions and behaviors but rarely wholly condemned them. It was something about his matter-of-fact expression. People are who they are and do what they do and perhaps that's too bad for others involved with them, but that was it. There was no belaboring the issues once he stated his observations. This Edith woman may have been some type of exception, as he mentioned her often, but even then, he was quite emotionally controlled.

For example, despite his direct and unceremonious chiding about the wrongs he believed she committed, Papa always held our mom to be a good person, which I believe ultimately helped him make peace with her decision. Her heart is good, and through all the discussions over the years that followed, I learned to recognize what Papa inferred was her ambivalence about leaving us. This was likely mitigated or at least rationalized somewhat by her consistent, almost daily contact with us. Papa always made it sound like she was looking for something that she was not even sure existed. I learned all this, I am certain that we all learned and understood this finally, allowing us to embrace our Mother just as he once did.

The arguments back and forth in the beginning often began with a discussion of some perceived need Mom had that something be done or said or bought and Papa's vociferous refusal based on, as he was sure to express in some way or another, her loss of rights to make such motherly decisions. He ultimately gave in, but by the time Mom left, she was exhausted and frustrated with his apparent need to put the energy into an argument with such frequency. These arguments were so disturbing that I made myself first deny the incidents and then forget them completely.

But my sisters remember more. Papa's eventual acceptance of her evident needs allowed her to relax as time went on, coming over whenever she wanted to, mostly unannounced. The fighting subsided and in time I think we all could see how it could be worse. Mom could be on drugs or alcoholic like we knew some children's parents were. Her categorical sense of responsibility, even if only perfunctory, had ensured her regular contact with us. There were no long periods of estrangement in terms of her total physical absence.

Bus Rides and a Turquoise Chevy

In 1957, we had a brand new automobile, a Chevy that only Mom could drive since Papa had evidently allowed his license to expire.

We once thought it possible that his purchase was merely another attempt to lure our Mom back to us. Papa had paid $4000.00 for his turquoise treasure and kept it in a locked garage down the street from our home.

Chevrolet is number one, he insisted, proud of his purchase.

Judging the value of a vehicle by the weight of its doors, Papa explained that cars made soon after our reliable Chevy were no longer being made with steel parts. Fuel-efficiency standards would require replacement parts like plastic and aluminum. Coming from a steelworker, this was a real shame; cars would never be the same again. Papa warned that the eventual 1,000-pound difference would truly be felt in any type of impact.

Papa was right about the cars. He would never buy another after his beloved Chevy. The 1973 energy crisis created the environment for smaller cars to be built to meet new fuel-efficiency standards, with the average 3,850 pounds in the mid-1970s to 2,800 pounds in the 1980s. The lighter materials like plastic and aluminum that replaced steel altered the value of the automobile, changed the industry and disappointed steelworkers like Papa.

Most weekends were an opportunity to see Mom, and that could be really nice if she was not crabby and emotionally loud and caused a raucous. Saturdays were usually reserved for grocery shopping at the Broadway Market, and we always knew that if Mom was joining us, we could get to ride in the prized Chevy and shop at Sattlers, 998

Broadway, the department store across the street from the Market. Mom always shopped until stores closed at 9pm, and although I do not have a clear recollection of what Papa was doing during those hours, he never seemed to display any impatience with her when it came to shopping with us. He'd simply show up at closing time somehow and we all departed together. Perhaps he was only too happy to have her spend time with the family.

On Sunday mornings, Mom came to call for us to attend Roman Catholic Mass. Papa resisted it at first, but eventually gave in to due to the discipline Catholic schools offered. At the time, attending Mass and being a Catholic was a prerequisite for attending the school.

Routine family trips had been established very early on so that we could be together, if even for those mundane treks of necessity. Food shopping at the local open-style market where everything edible could be bought and guaranteed fresh was a favorite weekly ritual. Papa would barter with the vendors at the Broadway Market located on the eastside, mostly Polish section, of Buffalo. When Mom was unable to take us in the car, Papa negotiated bus fares to get to the market for himself and his five children, justifiably obtaining a "volume discount."

Come on, come on, he'd insist to the driver, as he waived us ahead to be seated. *Five keet for one dolla, that's 'nuff*!

The bus drivers eventually gave in, although some did take longer than others. We never knew if they were somehow embarrassed into it or if they even ever had the latitude to 'deal' with a persistent negotiator who conveniently claimed to be unclear about what was being said to him in English. Nevertheless, Papa usually got his way with these guys.

Since we heard no one else conduct business in this manner, we assumed it was a throwback to our father's culture. It was a little distressing at times for us children, but no one else seemed to mind too much. I think they learned to expect it and accept it. Papa obviously spent a considerable amount of money with each of them every week, so I imagine he felt he had some negotiating leverage.

STATE OF NEW YORK
DEPARTMENT OF TAXATION AND FINANCE
BUREAU OF MOTOR VEHICLES

OPERATOR'S LICENSE

NOT VALID UNTIL DATED AND NUMBERED BY ISSUING OFFICE

License Number—Date of Issuance

(Do not write in this space)

EXPIRES SEPTEMBER 30, 1956

HAZIAM SALEH (Print or Type Full Name)

Street and No. 66 MYRTLE AVE (Give Legal Residence)

City or Post Office BUFFALO Zone No. 8 State N.Y.

Date of Birth Mo. Day Yr. 1900 — Color W — Sex M

Weight Lbs. — Height Ft. In. — Color of Eyes BROWN — Color of Hair BLACK

SPACES ABOVE TO BE FILLED IN BY APPLICANT

RESTRICTIONS:

Sign Your Name Above in Full — Not Initials

ANY ALTERATION EXCEPT ADDRESS VOIDS THIS LICENSE. THIS LICENSE IS RENEWABLE WITHOUT TESTS WITHIN ONE YEAR AFTER IT EXPIRES. LIST CHANGES OF ADDRESS ON OTHER SIDE M.V. 1

NOTIFY THIS BUREAU IN WRITING OF ANY CHANGE OF RESIDENCE WITHIN TEN DAYS AFTER SUCH CHANGE OCCURS

DO NOT DETACH

STATE OF NEW YORK
DEPARTMENT OF TAXATION AND FINANCE
BUREAU OF MOTOR VEHICLES

OPERATOR'S RENEWAL LICENSE STUB

TO BE PRESENTED WITH RENEWAL APPLICATION

License Number—Date of Issuance

(Do not write in this space)

ON OR BEFORE SEPTEMBER 30, 1956

HAZIAM SALEH (Print or Type Full Name)

Street and No. 66 MYRTLE AVE (Give Legal Residence)

City or Post Office — Zone No. — State N.Y.

Date of Birth Mo. Day Yr. 1900 — Color — Sex

Weight 135 Lbs. — Height 5 Ft. 5 In. — Color of Eyes — Color of Hair

SPACES ABOVE TO BE FILLED IN BY APPLICANT

RESTRICTIONS:

Sign Your Name Above in Full — Not Initials

IMPORTANT NOTICE: THIS RENEWAL LICENSE STUB MUST REMAIN ATTACHED UNTIL APPLICATION IS MADE FOR RENEWAL. ANY ALTERATION EXCEPT ADDRESS VOIDS THIS STUB. M.V. 1

REPORT ACCORDING TO LAW ANY ACCIDENT CAUSING INJURY TO A PERSON, A DOMESTIC ANIMAL, OR PROPERTY

DO NOT DETACH

Finding this was a surprise since I never saw Papa drive.

The predominately Polish market vendors and Papa knew one another by name and the owners seemed to look forward to our weekly visits. Our two largest purchases were meats from Redlinski's and dozens of the best soft rolls ever from Mrs.Cohen, the elderly white-haired baker lady. Mr. Redlinski, a name long recognized in the industry in town, understood Papa's need and insistence on hand-selection of steaks and the sirloin that would then be ground up for burgers. He would take no chances on any potential for the meats to be somehow mixed with or even touched by *khanzir*. And Papa spared no cost for food. It was always plentiful at our house; enough for us and for all our guests.

This weekly trip was an event for Papa. He put a great deal of energy and emphasis on the five of us joining him every Saturday. For years, we began in the early morning and returned home in the late afternoon or early evening. When Mom was with us, we would also sit down to eat at some point in that long shopping day, at one of the three restaurants on premise. One of our favorites was Mr. & Mrs. Pierson's place as it was right out in the open of the market rather than in an enclosed space. We all sat on swivel stools to eat and chat with the friendly owners. I was enamored with the Pierson's beautiful blue-eyed daughter, who was only in her twenties when she died in a horrible motorcycle accident. It affected me as if we had been related.

Mom would thrill us when she would come to the garage to fetch the Chevy and pile us all into the car for the ride to "Number 3 Gate." That was the door through which Papa emerged a free man after 8 to 16 hours (when he worked double shifts) of dirty, hard labor at the Bethlehem Steel Plant. This became one of the more regular family trips that car would make. On the way there, it was a fight for window seats; on the way back, it was who would get to sit near Papa.

One of the more memorable times in the Chevy with Papa had to do with his antics at the Canadian border when we had to encounter customs. As the inspectors proceeded through the car, they asked each of us:

Where were you born?

We are required to respond one-by-one: *Buffalo, United States*, as the officer looked us eye to eye, I guess, in search of incongruous body language.

Papa went last. It was another ritualistic event. He would flip open one side of his sport coat revealing a pocket filled with papers and a leather case. He would then reach into the compartment and pull out the long 3-part document containing his passport and naturalization papers. He would state as clearly as he was able, enunciating to ensure that he was understood:

I born in the United Arab Republic of Yemen as he unfolded, once, twice, three times, until the entire face of the document was revealed. I never knew if hc was more proud of his national heritage or the fact that he was an American citizen

ORIGINAL
TO BE GIVEN TO
THE PERSON NATURALIZED

No. 6664759

Petition No. 445282

50 years; sex Male
Dark Brown Black 5 feet 5 inches
weight 115 pounds; None
Married British

UNITED STATES OF AMERICA
EASTERN DISTRICT OF NEW YORK

District Court of The United States

Brooklyn

on August 13th 1946

HAZIAM SALEH

170 State Street, Brooklyn, New York

13th

August

forty-six

and seventy-first

U. S. District Court

The display tended to catch the inspectors by some surprise and at least pique their interest. Of course, it also meant a few extra minutes delay for review as well. Theatrics apparently came second nature to Papa, but it was unquestionable that he acquired and developed coping mechanisms to assist him with all he had to endure as he came along. And while Papa thoroughly enjoyed the audience, we children, anxious to arrive at our destiny, learned to anticipate transactions at the border with a degree of dread.

On most Sundays in the summertime, our prized 57 Chevy rode the family out to the country or for a day at the beach. Once in the town, we usually stopped to visit a farm that Papa had come to know. He and Mom both became friendly with the farmer and his wife, Mr. and Mrs. Bower, after stopping a number of years to purchase fresh fruit and eggs. Mrs. Bower could not seem to resist poking her large grey head into our car, coming almost nose-to-nose with one of us kids. She peered through her large clear plastic spectacles propping her face upward to ensure their position on her nose.

My, how you all keep growing!

And then,

So what grade are you in now, honey? She'd screech in her high-pitched singsong shaky voice that made me want to squint my eyes and bow my head into my chest until it stopped. It seemed she was always addressing *me* in particular, perhaps because she knew how much I loved school.

Speak up, my mother would chide, *she can't hear you when you mumble*.

But we knew the real reason why the old woman couldn't hear us. It was because she had a hearing problem! Truth is, Mrs. Bower rather gave me the creeps but she and her dear husband were really very kind, sweet people who were always good to my family.

As city kids, we were fascinated with the vastness of land out in the country and with the way farmers lived with chickens and hens and other animals everywhere. A cow named Molly was my personal favorite. I could never get over how close that big cow always seemed to come to the open door of their house. *Were they not concerned?* A homemade swing that hung from a huge Sycamore tree allowed me to enjoy many pendulant moments while my parents chatted with the old couple and my sisters and brother chased after the animals around the yard.

After our farm visit, it was off to Chestnut Ridge Park. There, we went to the highest peak and rolled ourselves all the way down the hill to where it was level. It usually took a while, with starts and stops to get realigned and continue in a downward, instead of lateral direction. Papa usually walked down so that he could be there once we all got to the bottom of the hill. Then, we would all climb back together, often stopping at a conveniently located shade tree to sit for a minute and catch our breath. Papa used to form contests of the activity to see who could roll the fastest or the straightest, ensuring that everyone won at least once. Then, back at the top, it was a visit to the indoor lodge, the "Casino," where we were able to use the bathrooms and get something to eat. We visited this park a few times in the winter season also, where we coasted down the snowy hills in toboggans.

Other Sundays we headed out to the beach as part of an Arabic caravan with one car following the other, all the way to Evangola State Park, about 20 miles south of our house in the city. There were six to eight cars filled with people, most of whom were related. We were the odd family, in the sense that we were *not* related, and we were not "traditional," particularly by Arabic standards. By that time, everyone knew that although our mother drove us and came with us as a family, she had not been living with us.

When Papa had to work, he would join us at the site once his shift ended, provided he could get a ride out there. The five of us were like a bunch of shipwrecked orphans treading water until Papa arrived and we were able to swim to safety. That is how it felt, in retrospect. *Where is Papa?* Our baby sister would ask. *He'll be here soon,* someone would say to comfort her. *Where is Papa?* I thought so often. *When will he be here*? *Please hurry*, anxious that he would not show because he was unable to get a ride—it just wasn't possible to get there by bus—or that he had to work overtime. Invariably, he made it and my siblings and I could finally exhale. It was always much better then. Papa was devoted to us, paid attention to us and made sure that we had anything we wanted to eat. His arrival assured our comfort, our inclusion in the group, our right to be there.

Even after mom left and especially after the dust had settled, we all enjoyed our time together. For me, it was an opportunity to pretend we were just like any other family. In looking back, I see how it might have been Papa's patience that created and allowed for the possibility. Whatever it took to get us to spend time together was something he delighted in, no matter how it would go. I rather doubt that he was always having such a good time, especially enduring the long shopping hours that mom certainly enjoyed, but I think it was okay and I can not remember a moment of tension associated with these experiences. The times that were anxiety-ridden, times when mom came to our house and there were disagreements and heated discussions, were private matters, never public displays. The most that might take place publicly is that Papa might tease mom, an expression of his humor that she'd rarely appreciate, when her frustrated response was an ambivalent, *Oh, comon', Saleh*!

******

It has continued to amaze me that Papa always pined for Mom, wanting always for her return and never completely losing hope. The fact is that they were rather opposite, in temperament as well as in many of their goals and values. Where Papa was simple, Mother was complex and sometimes confusing. Where Papa was straightforward, Mom danced around subjects and evaded questions. Mother was busy doing things, restless about life and seeking greener pastures. Papa was content to work, eat, sleep, and take care of his children. Mom placed a great deal of emphasis on material things; Papa called anything more than the essentials a total waste of money. In the home, Mom was obsessive about cleanliness when Papa was not at all fussy. And although Papa consistently treated people with respect and consideration, he could not care less what other people thought or said. This was one of mother's preoccupations. *What would people say*? She'd ask frequently. *So what?* Was Papa's retort, spoken and unspoken. What I have learned is that love does not necessarily involve logic.

Combined, their strengths obviously balanced our daily life as Papa was the one to keep us fed and sheltered while mom took care of the details of our education, better clothing and extracurriculars. In other words, Papa was more about needs while mom took care of the wants, but in a sense, it worked out perfectly for this divided and broken family. Unfortunately, when mom decided to leave her family, the relationship had to end, but the love never would. That fact was a lesson to all of us on the meaning of unconditional love and acceptance.

******

A Father's Age

Because of Papa's advanced age, we would on occasion encounter vendors at the marketplace and others who presumptuously referred to him as our "grandfather." Very often our response was "*he is not our grandfather; he is our father!*" It was a protective, defensive posture. It never bothered Papa, but it invariably evoked an annoyed response from each of his children at one time or another.

It was as if most people with whom we initially came in contact could hardly resist their curiosity. We came to understand that Americans had often used the term "Papa" to mean grandfather. Perhaps once people realized that he was an "older" father virtually raising five children on his own, ranging seven years from eldest to the youngest, who was just a toddler when it all began, they may have been struck with sadness, wonder, possibly even pity, as there had been frequent expressions of indulgence from friends as well as strangers.

Still, while our status could have been the reason for the many people who were good to us, I have difficulty envisioning anyone feeling pity for Papa. I have always chosen to believe that people were nice to our father because he treated them with kindness and courtesy and the fact that he raised particularly well-behaved children only added to his appeal.

Other people's 'judgment' of Papa's age must have affected me, however. I felt cheated and often sad, even ashamed of having a father old enough to be the parent of some of my friends' parents. But once I was well into my twenties, I realized that none of that mattered. I came to realize that a good father was priceless at any age. He was infinitely better than a 'bad' young father or no father at all, I told myself. And there was always the obvious benefit of the wisdom of an older parent that cannot be underestimated.

Age did not seem to rob Papa of much energy, at least not while we were very young and he was still working. During summers when we could play outside all day, Papa would try to work the late shift. *I work steady nights,* he'd tell us, meaning that he would work the 11PM to 7AM, a shift that allowed him to spend his days sitting on the front porch, watching us play kick ball or tag on the street for hours and hours.

Those times were the only ones we got to remain outdoors after the streetlights came on. Once we went in for the night, we ate dinner and called the order for our baths. Papa or my sister Delilah would prepare for his work day by making his lunch, usually egg or tuna sandwiches, and when we were still hiring them, babysitters arrived to stay the night. But there was nothing much they had to do. It was a late hour and Papa had thought of everything.

Of course when the physical challenges did begin to manifest, the first thing we considered was his age. For example, when Papa fell off the chair in the kitchen and broke his ribs. He had a habit of stepping onto a chair in order to retrieve something in a cabinet up high, despite my mother's repeated warnings. The doctors bound his entire chest area and kept it that way for a long time. Papa didn't complain and he was more or less compliant, but the site of that bounding was a sobering reminder that something worse could always happen.

When I was sixteen, I had taken a job in a Catholic hospital kitchen located just a short bus ride from my high school on Main Street. It was my first real job, after babysitting and ironing for a prominent local family with nine children. Neither of my parents had ever asked me nor expected me to work but they expressed pride in my efforts. I enjoyed having my own money and even ended up helping mom pay my tuition. Papa urged me to "same my money," rather than *spend it foolishly*, but he left me to manage myself. At St Francis Hospital, I came in contact with motherly and grandmotherly women, such as Irene and Helen, with whom I would confide about my girlfriend problems and immature love life. Meeting in the locker room before punching in on the work card and whatever chances we would get on the job, I could hear their sage advice as they related tales of when they were my age and had similar experiences.

While preparing for patients' meals one spring afternoon, I had the unfortunate experience of having my chest burned with scalding hot water. I had been approaching rapidly in one direction to place a pot for tea onto a dinner tray at the same time that another girl was hurrying in the opposite direction. We collided, which caused the pot to pop open and spill up and back onto me. I was shocked and hurt but immediately treated by the hospital doctors. The worst thing was that I happened to be performing in a school play and I was extremely upset about the huge piece of white gauze that was surely going to show in my low cut costume the very next evening. It was Kaufman's comedy, *You can't take it with You* and I was playing the drunken actress wearing a rather low-cut dress. It had been challenging enough as I was nervous about acting in a role in which I had no experience and *now this*.

Soon after my incident, Papa's doctor had convinced him to have a cataract operation in the very hospital where I worked. The surgery was scheduled just after the school year ended, the same time when my own hours had been increased for the summer. On that day, as soon as I arrived just on time for work, I changed into my uniform and quickly ran to tell the other workers about my father. I was going to check on him and would be down immediately after. I checked for the room number, ran all the way up the two flights of stairs to avoid waiting for the elevator, and excitedly entered the room. What I saw was Papa sitting on the bed with what seemed like an enormous white gauze on his one eye. I was not prepared for this; the moment I saw him I made a complete turn to exit and immediately burst into tears.

A medical professional caught sight of me in the hallway and ran over to determine how he might help. This man was very reassuring and I recall him explaining that I could not let my father know that I was upset; it would not be good for him to see me cry, etc. After a short time, I composed myself and reentered the room for my visit but in the end, Papa consoled me. *It's nothing. Come, come.*

The more conscious I became of his advanced age, the greater was the fear of losing him. I liked it better when I hardly got that or when I could still be in denial. When I heard that a man down the street had a heart attack shoveling snow, I added snow removal surveillance every time Papa went outside to clear the snow from our path, which was probably too often for a man his age. Buffalo and snow are synonymous and in the harsh winters of my childhood, I prayed that it would stop because I knew Papa would not. Whenever he had a minor run in with someone, like the young men he did not want talking to his daughters or the people he preferred not park in front of our house even as they worked nearby and had every right, it was always a scare that something sometime would go wrong. It may not have been the wisest move, but Papa never backed down from anyone. *Whassa matter with you, I no scare!*

*No, Papa, I know that you're not scared, but **I** am.*

I do not think my feelings would have been exactly as they were had he been a younger man.

Like other experiences outside my home, my life at the hospital was another venue for my ongoing American education. I spoke to and listened much to the words of the older women who ran the hospital kitchen. When I had my problems with my schoolmates and couldn't figure it out, one of them would explain how some girls could actually be jealous of my relationship with my boyfriend, my good grades, or both. They spoke with authority, reinforced my father's values, which I liked because it made me feel that his rules weren't all that odd. These older and wiser women talked about life and love and loss and I remember thinking that they certainly sounded like they knew things I did not and that I needed to listen to them because maybe they were trying to have me learn from what they have lived, to sort of lessen the intensity of my more difficult lessons. After all, they had no agenda, no reason to lie to me or even to help me. And like my own parents and even siblings, they respected the fact that I worked to help pay for my Catholic education.

In my adult years, I began to worry about Papa's smoking habit. I had not thought of it too much growing up; it was just something Papa did. But the awareness of lung damage added to his exposure at the steel plant and made me increasingly uneasy. Every time he took out a smoke, which in reality was less and less often as he grew older, I braced myself in order not to admonish my own father about his health. We even purchased an area piece made of asbestos to cover the carpet around the chair in which he often sat to smoke, but we soon discovered what a bad idea that was. It was not a long time after when Papa began to experience more regular periods of poor health and on his good days I would just want him to have whatever he wanted if he enjoyed it and that unfortunately included cigarettes. I was not without ambivalence on the matter, however, and was regularly chided by my siblings who thought otherwise.

******

When it came to traveling to visit Mom's family, Papa was compliant and even generous. In earlier years, we took the seven and a half-hour train ride to Grand Central Station with our mom, then a local subway from there to ultimately arrive in Brooklyn, where we would visit for weeks in the summer. In later years, we would take a plane, or as my mom would refer to it back then, "a jet." Brooklyn was the setting for my introduction and developed expertise in advanced jump rope or "Double Dutch" as it is called, and where I was initiated into the idea of cooling off via urban water sprinklers, compliments of the street fire hydrants. It was a routine affair—seemed to be accepted although technically illegal.

Life was indeed different in Brooklyn. If Papa had known all we were exposed to, I am not so sure that we would have been permitted to go, but other than asking how everyone in the family was doing, he never asked what we did while we were there. Apparently when I was only 3 and a half years old and still in a stroller, Henry, my step grandfather, and my Uncle Mike, partners in a bar, got into a fight over money. Delilah, only five years old, remembers us outside the bar door, railroad tracks to the left, and she hears yelling and screaming. She looks over, eyes growing wide because she sees someone grabbing a knife and while our Mom tries unsuccessfully to convince them not to fight, someone called the police and it was bedlam. Delilah remembers being terrified and she was either too afraid to tell Papa or was told not to, but I am relatively certain that he never found out about the incident.

Another time, when I was only sixteen years old, my 21 year-old cousin Mitchell took me for a car ride into the city late at night. I was impressed with the big beautiful buildings, which I could only now appreciate, without my mom hastily whisking me in and out of New York and now that all the people were out of the way. It was a magical night for me, getting to go deep into Central Park to meet up with a number of Mitchell's friends, them teasing about us being "cousins" and him showing me the ropes around town. It had to have been late into the night, perhaps one or two in the morning, when we returned to Brooklyn. As Mitchell pulled the car up to let me out, I looked up and saw my Grandmother in the window. *Grandma*, I said. *What are you still doing up*?

I am waiting for you.

Oh, you didn't have to wait for me, Grandma. I'm all right. See!?

You are all right, she admonished, waving her finger at me. *But,*

***I** am not!*

I'd never forget her expression that night. I laughed but it wasn't very funny. My poor aging grandmother felt responsible and concerned and that had kept her up well beyond her bedtime. With that, she went away from the window to see me into the house. Once again, I assumed that Papa never heard of that incident, as it may well have ended my summer visits to Brooklyn.

Changes in the Neighborhood

By the time I graduated from eighth grade, our neighborhood had changed from middle class to a lower middle class area. It marked a dramatic shift in terms of the friends with whom we were allowed to play. Most of our good friends were the first to move, which meant that we could stay out less and less time. It also meant that our dog had to become a real watchdog. Papa made certain that Duke could watch over us while he was working. He had trained him in his own way, commanding him in Arabic mostly, fully capitalizing on a German Shepherd's nature to be protective. We had had him as a newborn puppy, but at some point in the neighborhood's deterioration, Duke was stolen. We were crushed. Papa interpreted this gesture as a ploy to ensure that our house and his children would remain defenseless while he worked, leaving us vulnerable to an intended and uninterrupted robbery.

We decided to place an ad in the paper offering a monetary reward for Duke's safe return and hoped that would do the trick to get our dog back home. Soon after, a young boy came forward for the money, but asked us to promise that his identity would not be revealed. He was concerned for his safety and so were we. We paid the boy, called the police and retrieved our dog in the basement of a house that lay adjacent to the garage we had been renting for our car.

The two black men who were responsible had starved Duke and kept him blindfolded. One of the policemen told us that starving a dog was a tactic used to produce anger and therefore attack behavior. Who knew what plans these thieves had? But as far as we could determine, the only thing it succeeded in doing was to get Duke to hate anyone who was black after that incident. Nonetheless, our darling German Shepherd proved to be the best watchdog ever.

******

Mom left at the end of the 1950s, just when the social climate was getting tense. The way she explains it, by the mid 1960s, *the civil rights movement allowed blacks and whites to live side by side*. This meant, of course, that restrictions had been lifted that had prevented blacks from moving into "white neighborhoods." The talk was that the black people who moved in were not taking care of their property in our neighborhood, causing the whites, mostly the "Italians," but also some Irish and Polish who had been the majority home owners, to move out further into the suburbs, mostly south of Buffalo. As properties depreciated, more homes became affordable to those who would not care for them and it just spiraled downward. Why did they not take care of their homes? The only answer I was able to get from people of this period was that these often first time homeowners had no idea how to care for property since they had little to no experience doing so.

"The Great Society" of the 1960s under President Johnson, was the Civil Rights Legislation. Folks demonstrated and demanded their human rights and were angered by the violent and unjust deaths of some leaders, such as Martin Luther King, who called attention to the injustices. His positive influence had been cut short with his life taken by a white man. Then Bobby Kennedy was assassinated and he was thought to be a champion of civil rights, adding fuel to the fire.

The movement also ended the unlocked door policy at Markel Electric where mom was employed at the time. Mom remembers this as the beginning of the end of the kind of trust that permitted people to feel non-threatened, free of concern. To feel the kind of safety that allows one to live without having to think about locking doors to cars and homes. The potential for riots and demonstrations that could end in violence was a reality and she, for one, was becoming more and more fearful.

Almost any incident became another reason to reinforce the need to move from the neighborhood but Papa was resistant and used our absent mother as one explanation for his reluctance. The few times Papa considered moving, we had gone to see houses and he was amazed at the prices.

What, are they crazy, ask this kind money for house?

Papa thought the going rates for homes at the time ought to buy you a mansion on the most expensive block in the city. We didn't dare even approach the suburbs for fear of what they would ask for a home that would accommodate a rather large family. After an evening of house hunting, Papa would acknowledge my visible signs of frustration.

You see, if your mother was with us, I buy another house. But for what now?

I would think about that over and over again, wondering if he really expected that I had any control over my mother's actions.

Even though Mom lived nearby, only a few blocks away, she lived on a block that had just three homes on it. On the corner was a nice tavern in a gorgeous old building and between the two houses and a third home, there was a long stretch of a sterile-looking wax factory. On the opposite side of the street were railroad tracks. What this really meant was that the house she lived in was unaffected by the direction in which the area was seemingly headed. The commercial aspect of her block kept "unfavorable" tenants at a distance, and the businesses were all very tidy. It would be awhile before mom would need to move from that street.

My repeated attempts to get Papa to move continued to be met with disappointment. Although the other children were excited about the prospect, I often felt completely alone in my struggling initiative toward this objective. I somehow got drafted into position of vanguard for the family's safe and prideful living quarters, to say nothing of the cosmetic, albeit superficial issues dictated by peer influence. Since I had difficulty surrendering my cause without a fight, I delayed college one semester after I graduated high school, believing I could help Papa purchase a new home for us. I felt confident and capable, even though I was only being paid minimum wage as a full-time clerk in an insurance company.

But even when I got closer to gaining a sincere interest from Papa, I could never get him past the dollar amount we would have to pay for the house. I even tried to make a deal with the real estate agent to misinform Papa. To tell him that the house was less than it was. But that proved to be too difficult. I knew that I would have to be involved in all the paper work as a "cosigner," so I figured we might manage to keep the details away from Papa. Since it was the summer before my 18th birthday, we were even going to wait to put the paper work through in the following couple of months.

I had my heart set on one house in particular, a very large white house on Voorhees, a well-groomed street in north Buffalo. It was big enough for each of us to have our own bedroom. There was more than one bathroom and a large backyard that even appealed to Papa. As we toured the house, I tried not to show how excited I was, so as not to discourage my father from saying exactly what he felt. As we exited the house, we said goodbye to the realtor. She smiled and winked at me.

Good Luck, she whispered. I could hardly contain myself as I felt my heart racing. I thought, *how could Papa say no*? It was all we would ever want. And I will help to pay for it. I don't care if I never get to go to college!

But, it would never happen. We left the house, and as we walked down the street, Papa said it was too expensive. Since he was already retired, he was living on a fixed income. What if we needed extra money for something, you know, that "rainy day" that older folks were always talking about. *And what about* (*my) school*?

You want be ticher, Papa reminded me. *How you work and go school, too? Maybe if you mother come...*

I was devastated as I listened to him, all the way home on the bus. I failed to convince him once again. That's when I knew my fight was probably over.

Maybe Papa really wanted me to blame my mother by now, as he reminded me so often of a time when I was still very young and asked him, *When are we going to get another mother?* Maybe he thought he had been too kind to her and about her all these years. He had never alienated us in any real way, and he continued to allow her to visit anytime; there were no restrictions. But I could not possibly understand how or why we were entitled to a new home contingent on our mother's returning home. The inferences were entirely frustrating to me as a teenager. It never made me madder at her; it only made me angry at him.

I was angry that he could not understand how important it was to me and my brother and sisters. How great it would be to have space. How sincere I was about helping out. How my sisters, brother and I would rather be in a good neighborhood and be able to stay outdoors a little than never get to go out after dark. It was evident that Papa was not one for risks, however. He lived conservatively, all the way. I would have to just accept that.

Haircuts and High School

Even in smaller ways, cultural separateness continued to surface in our daily lives such as Papa's forbidding my sisters and me to cut our very long hair. I once went to a five and dime store with my high school girlfriends and got my hair cut like I had no business doing, not so much because of Papa, but because this very short haircut was intended for girls with straight, soft, fine, *thinner* hair. Still, when everyone else was doing it, my desire to be "in style" won out over my common sense. Because of its curl and coarseness, it puffed up at the top and made it look like I was wearing some kind of a 1950s pill hat that had 2 side springs, one attached to each cheek, pretending to be spit curls at either end. I had to tape down those sides at night and was so fearful of revealing my twiggy haircut to Papa that I wore a scarf in the house for an entire week. I was managing that all right until the day Papa's suspicions motivated him to pull the scarf right off my head from behind me. He was upset by my defiance; he said "Arabic girls" did not follow American fashion. I looked so ugly that I wanted to admit to Papa that I wished I had listened. That was the beginning of a very long year.

In my father's country, once a girl completed her education (we are talking high school, usually) she married and had children. As my older sister and I neared that age, my father suggested to us that he could arrange a marriage through his people. Somehow both Delilah and I came close to going through with it. In the end when it did not come to pass, we were happier and Papa never said much about it. I guess he realized that we were American girls, after all, wanting to live the American life with marriage itself not even a necessary objective.

Delilah remembers at least two men who came to call for her with offers of marriage. The first came with gold jewelry. Delilah was around 16 years of age and the man about 30. After some discussion with Papa, the man left the jewelry. Delilah was impressed and tried on the beautiful shiny gold bracelets. Even back then, the typical gold from the Middle East is generally of a higher carat quality than most gold bought in the U.S. She marveled at the pieces, thrilled that someone wanted to give her *such beautiful things*. Then Papa explained.

This man, he want marriage with you.

Delilah was surprised but not immediately alarmed. She wanted to understand. Papa continued.

You no need work; somebody take care of you for your life.

If she accepted the jewelry, Papa said, she accepted the offer of marriage.

Delilah did not have to think about this.

No, Papa. I don't even know this man. This ended the proposition and somehow Papa returned the jewelry.

But apparently, Papa did not think that the matter was closed.

The next time, a short time after, with Delilah around the same age, perhaps closer to 17 years of age, she remembers that the man was a bit older than the first. He too came with jewelry and a gift for Papa.

This time Delilah refused the jewelry up front and stepped away from Papa and the man who were still in discussion. She is clear now, speaking plainly and directly. After the man left, Delilah said:

Stop having these men come here, Papa. Don't bring any more men in here to marry me because I'm ***not*** *going to do it.*

Papa seemed a little dejected but he let it be. Delilah feels that she let him down, disappointed Papa for the rest of his life because she did not marry an Arab. As it turned out, she never married anyone.

About a year later, Delilah had a mild crush on another Arab from Jordan who ended up returning to his home. He was handsome and nice enough but somehow we all knew that it was not right. But then another man came to visit. He was the nephew of a friend of Papa's, an Arab from Ethiopia whom Papa would refer to as "Somali line." His name was Yousef and Delilah really liked this man, found him to be *truly a nice person,* exceptionally interesting and intelligent. He was enrolled at the University of Buffalo and told Delilah that his goal was to work for the UN. To this day, she regrets losing contact with this man because she believed he genuinely liked her and she may have even considered marrying him. But Papa had discouraged this prospect. He did not want Delilah to end up with him, saying only that he was *too dark*. Many years later, when Delilah and I spoke about this, we decided that knowing Papa as we did, it had to be something we did not understand that caused him to not be in favor of her being with this perfectly lovely individual.

When it came time for me, once I turned 16, Papa wanted to check my receptivity and spoke in general about the idea of an arranged marriage.

No, Papa, I don't think so, Is what I remember. It's not that I thought it was a horrible idea, I just could not imagine it. Careful not to hurt his feelings, I was not so direct and terminal.

We spoke a bit more, about the philosophy, his intent, all of which I was certain was simply for my own good, but I could never imagine my life as an Arab's wife. I knew what I knew and that role just did not feel right. After all, in most ways, I was a typical teenage American girl.

Then I met someone. It was the summer before I turned 16. He was related to one of my father's friends from Palestine. The first day we met I remember thinking *now this one I could marry*. He was more than handsome, had a great personality and the chemistry was as perfect as one might imagine. I was head over heels and Papa knew it.

You are love? He asked me.

That was Papa's embarrassingly straightforward questioning on being "in love." I did not answer right off. I took a moment to think of how exactly to respond.

Cause if you are love, then you marry.
Oh, it all was so black and white to Papa.

Thabet came to call on me a number of times and we sat on my porch to talk under my father's watchful eye. We went out alone only a few times and they were all during the days and usually with someone else accompanying us. To be alone, we decided we would meet each morning at the bus stop on Delaware Avenue. For me it was the interim step between the second bus I had to get for school and he just walked over from his west side home. He was on his way to work. There we took time to hug and kiss and talk and basically proclaim our love for each other in the cold and the rain and wind.

In the end, Thabet and I would be separated by expectation. He was almost 10 years older than I was and would soon want to marry. His parents preferred one directly from Palestine and I wanted to attend college and obtain an education—it would be years before I would even think of marriage.

I attended Thabet's wedding with Papa and a few of my siblings, a few years later. I followed my father in, nervously walking up to the marriage table, which faced you as you walked into the prominent old structure on Delaware Avenue, just a few blocks from our little store front bus stop, where we had spent so much time professing our love. *Congratulations*, I said to her and then to him. She seemed to stare at me.

Was she really staring, had he told her about me, or was this merely my active imagination?

I talked Papa into not staying too long. I don't think I breathed until I exited that building. Papa was quiet. I thought he knew exactly how I felt and I was definitely grateful that we weren't going to have a conversation.

Many years later, a cousin of his was getting married and as usual, my family was invited. I remember standing in line for the buffet wondering whether he would be attending this celebration, since he had long relocated to Florida and was self-employed in the grocery business. Before me in line were two very young girls, giggling and talking away when one of my sisters asked the little girl if they were sisters.

Yes, she said. *There are five of us.*

Wow, we thought, as she pointed toward her siblings nearby, all appearing very close in age.

Who is your father? We asked.

Him, said the one little girl, probably the oldest. My eyes turned to follow her pointed arm. It was *him!* I just knew it. Five little girls. Amazing, I thought, as that same weird feeling came over me that I had the day of his wedding.

I do not know if Papa's dreams for us to marry in his custom were devastating losses, because he never really let on that they were. Clearly, my dreams were at the expense of his, perhaps the same for all my sisters. He actually liked that I was going to college and getting a teaching degree, and he spoke of me to others with pride. He believed that I selected an admirable and respectable profession. And I believe that once I set the stage, the fact that my sisters continued with their education did please him. Still, unlike Mom, who remained adamant about our education, Papa had only modest career expectations for all his children. As long as we were happy and were able to take care of ourselves and our family, that was all that mattered. He thought it was good to have an education, and he was proud when we achieved there, but it was never necessary. It is true that he did have an influence both in my choice to move into business and in my ultimate decision to leave because it was more about trial and error and accepting and rejecting opportunities. The self-confidence and discipline that he instilled in me gave me the courage to believe that I could do what I wanted, mindful of a quality of life, my personal life—even if I did have to marry an *American*.

With manifestly high principals, Papa remained vitally opinionated, obstinate as a father could be and fairly inflexible, so as an adolescent who thought she'd die if she did not get to do what other girls did, I had learned to lie to get to do things that my friends did. I began to work on Papa several days before I wanted to attend an event or party. Once, I was in a panic about going to a date dance during high school. I was the president of my class that year, and felt it was necessary that I be there. But I had two problems: Papa, who would never understand the entire affair *(Whas kind dence, are you crazy?)* and I had no boyfriend, neither of which I had wanted to admit to. First, I decided, along with a few cohorts, to send a typed letter to my home, requesting my presence at the Sophomore Date Dance and "signed" by one of the nuns. My accomplices, three girlfriends, all helped to formulate the wording, get it typed, forged, and mailed. We apparently did such a fine job that I did get to go to that dance—chaperoned, of course. (I went with a boy who was a friend and just happened to be gorgeous.) I have often wondered, did Papa really know what was going on? There are times when I suspect that I failed to fool him but he let me go anyway. I have felt badly about that lie. It was a very (American) "teenage" thing to do.

For me, high school had represented more than the next hurdle in my academic education; it was a social education, as well, a real departure from my neighborhood schooling experience. I took two buses to attend the all-girls, largely middle class Catholic High School, Bishop O'Hern, on Main Street in Buffalo. The lovely old buildings that made up the campus had history, both as an orphanage and a home for unwed mothers before becoming a high school. When I first arrived, I was generally surprised at the level of "exposure" other girls had at the time, though I feel certain I was not alone. It seemed most girls had had boyfriends, both before and during the first year I showed up at age 13, turning 14 that October. Some had probably already experienced sex. They wore makeup and shaved their legs and plucked their eyebrows. I felt I had a great deal of catching up to do but I was not pressured, only mildly teased. There was still a sort of quiet respect at the time for girls like me. You easily heard distinguishing references to young women as "sluts" and "easy" and I just knew I did not want to be *that*. Like the others, I was concerned about my body weight but my primary source of self-consciousness would be my hair. In those days, I was still trying to manage it or more specifically, control it. I tried ironing and setting my big hair in enormous rollers that I slept in—very uncomfortably. It was before the days anyone would wisely advise, "Make peace with your hair (the way it is naturally)," "learn to live with it," and "it's great, many would like to have it."

I can recall one night, when after I begged my father to allow me to sleep over at the school's pajama party, the girls took me on as a project, tweezing my eyebrows and showing me how to shave my legs. They even applied makeup to my face but they may have overdone it because I remember looking in the mirror afterward and thinking *No, Papa would not like this at all* but *I* even thought I looked bad. Moreover, it *felt* really awful so I washed it off as soon as I could.

By sophomore year, I guess I was growing in popularity because I was elected class president. I had not dated just yet but by the end of the year I would be in love with my Arabic guy and then within another year I had met my first 'real' American boyfriend. He attended Fallon, the all-boys Catholic school across the street.

I hid Paul from Papa for as long as I could but one day, when Papa caught him walking me to my door after we had ridden the bus together to my home, I pulled out all the stops to 'sell' Papa on this nice boy who worked at a gas station while going to school and knew all about cars.... *Isn't that interesting*!?

Papa gave me a hard time anyway. It was a battle of wills because I felt so strongly that I was right. I did nothing wrong, only had a boyfriend. I thought him unreasonable because it was all so innocent. He obviously did not trust me (or the boy or both) and I didn't want to defend my self or talk about it, I just wanted to run away.

What I once perceived to be Papa's relentless impositions of principle and discipline resulted in the two of us having terrible disagreements. Meeting a boy during my second year of high school only worsened our tensions at home and when one of my sisters saw me holding hands and kissing him goodbye, she squealed faster than I could think to bribe her not to tell. For a time after, it was very difficult for Papa and me to be in the same room.

Sometime during the following school year, it got decided that I would go live with my Catholic godmother, the same woman that Papa had associated with Mom's departure. Papa had warned that if I left I could not return home but he would not stop me. I did not take much, only a few uniforms, white regulation blouses, some shoes, books and a few other articles. I do not recall much about being there, only that I got to spend innocent time with my boyfriend and that I had my own bedroom. My sisters were glad that I left. They thought I was selfish and mean, which I probably was, but I did not see that then. I was surprised that Papa would rather have me live away rather than compromise his principles or have me "influence" my sisters.

Living at Edith's home was good and bad. I felt the estrangement from my family and my father's disappointment but I enjoyed the private bedroom and freedom of what I thought was a more "normal" situation. My teenage selfishness overrode any real guilt or emotional attachment I had had—at least for a time. At Edith's, my responsibilities were limited to keeping my room clean and doing my homework. The best part was that my boyfriend was allowed to visit and phone me freely. Paul even rode the buses with me just to spend time, having to turn right back around and make the long return trip to his home. The biggest inconvenience was that I was living in Hamburg, way south of the city and I often came from work, way north. It took two buses to get home, one all the way down Main Street into downtown Buffalo and the transfer bus all the way down South Park Avenue into Hamburg. Luckily there were accommodating bus schedules but it still meant spending at least two hours on buses back and forth. One time on the way home I fell asleep and had to repeat the route, making it rather late and very inconvenient. Edith was not happy. It had been some time since she had had any responsibility for a child as her own was now in her twenties and already married. She was nice but stern about it and I made sure I never did that again.

Papa and I would eventually work things out once I sort of agreed not to have a boyfriend, knowing that I could see Paul everyday anyway. He was at school almost directly across the street from where I was so we could meet each morning for breakfast at the near-by Your Host restaurant before classes. After school and on days that I worked, he would cross the street to walk over to meet me in front of O'Hern to board the bus with me and get off a couple of stops before I did. Sometimes on his evenings off his gas station job he would meet me after I worked and we would spend just a little time before I went home. Resolution with Papa was not yet complete, however.

My sisters said that it was quiet after I left. I guess it was better for everyone since I was caught up in my selfish teenage-ness and not very fun to be around. I would not remember missing anyone. Papa would ask my siblings questions about me and have them call me to check in regularly but I remained there almost an entire school semester without ever seeing my father.

I never really knew what Papa thought of my time living with my Godmother—I did know that I could not resolve in my mind how he was feeling about not being able to keep track of me anymore and what he may have been going through given our on going struggles with me and boys. I knew only that he was firm on his opinion and leaving was a lot easier than staying and arguing about it.

As time went on, Papa seemed to recede in his Arab ness, allowing his children in their full-fledged *American-ness* to do as Americans do, with some distinct exceptions. By the time we were all adolescents, most of us attending high school at the same time, we were engaged in the same dance our peers were to distance ourselves from our parents. Those four years almost seemed to function as cementing the groundwork for what we were to become in life, taking up where we left off in the developmental years back in grade school. But this period served as the "coming of age" of the more social kind, when we thought we were nearly full-fledged men and women. Papa often watched and listened intently without saying too much, but always, *always*, one step ahead of us.

I remember reading a quote from Mark Twain that described how I felt in retrospect about these silly offenses with Papa:

When I was a boy of fourteen, my father was so ignorant I could hardly stand to have the old man around. But, when I got to be twenty-one, I was astonished at how much the old man had learned in seven years."

******

It was indeed just about the time that I turned fourteen years of age when I began to discover that there was a whole other world out there. Attending an all-girls school would never shelter me completely from the opposite sex. In fact, the all-boys Catholic school a stone's throw from ours allowed me to peek at many of the cute guys when I boarded the two metro buses traveling to and from Bishop O' Hern High School every day. I thought Papa was way out of line with all his rules and insistence on no boy friends. I was all grown up. I wanted to have a boyfriend. After all, I was so mature and responsible. He had no right to interfere. Like Mark Twain said, he just was ignorant. I did not care how long he had been living here. He did not understand me, or *the way things were in America.*

On my very first day of high school, there was an orientation held for freshmen in the gym, which also served as an auditorium. We were to be welcomed, get our assignments, and head to the bookstore to pick up supplies. Papa had arrived along with me to school that morning. He said he just wanted to be sure I took the right buses and got off at the correct stop. He also said that he would like to introduce himself to the *sistas*. I did cringe, but really did not say too much, kissing him goodbye and making my way though the morning and finally into orientation. I rather believed that Papa was determined to confirm that I was indeed attending an all-girls school and to ensure his approval of the overall environment. I was confident that it would meet with his approval.

By the time I got there, the auditorium was filled with over one hundred girls and several faculty members (all of whom were female and the majority of whom were nuns). Suddenly, I heard one of the girls in a loud whisper: *There's a man in the back of the room*! I quickly turned to look and there stood my father at the rear of the aud, taking it all in. I wondered how long he had been standing there. I had thought that by this time he had spoken to the school Principal and been well on his way home. I was embarrassed. I felt like a little girl whose father was checking up on her. I yielded an inconspicuous wave and went about my business. Papa eventually left.

In four years, I had matured some, though not much. But this time I was touched, and at least able to appreciate the generosity of my father's love. It was graduation day. The ceremony was relatively formal, consistent with Roman Catholic practice. Since it was to take place inside of St. Joseph's Cathedral, I accepted that Papa would not enter. He was always willing to go just so far with this religion thing, and going inside a Catholic Church was too far. There could be no compromise.

As my class paraded by the many onlookers, I caught sight of a few family members. But in the midst of so much anticipation, I really did not know who was there. Once in the church, however, everyone including me, searched for our families. Flashes from the numerous cameras came from everywhere. All of a sudden, I heard one of my classmates exclaim: *Mr. Saleh's here*! Most of my friends knew about my father; they realized that this was a monumental event. I looked back, and there he was again. Standing quietly at the back of the church, with my mom, taking it all in. I smiled at him and then I waved. My heart was touched as no one could have known. *Thanks,*

Papa. I could never have appreciated that enough. It was an unforgettable day, and it became an even more unforgettable night.

In the excitement following graduation exercises, I somehow managed to get my father's consent to celebrate with my friends. A group of us had made an impromptu decision to take a few carloads of people and head out to Niagara Falls. I cheerfully made my way to one of the cars and gestured an enthusiastic goodbye to my family.

For the first time in my life, I had not given any thought to what time I should be home, and for the first time, I neglected to ask. Perhaps a subconscious attempt to claim ignorance, but it all happened just too quickly and I had obviously taken advantage of the moment.

When my friends and I finally arrived at Niagara Falls, we really didn't have a clue what to do, so we did a lot of nothing. It was a silly, fun time, and it was entirely innocent. A time any parent could readily sanction.

As time flies when you're having fun, however, it was about four o'clock in the morning before any of us cared to look. In a moment of temporary seriousness, we all agreed that I should be the first to be dropped off. The long ride home was interchangeably mixed with an uneasy silence and nervous laughter. I knew that my friends were concerned for me and were doing their best to keep the mood light. As the three cars pulled up to the curb, I got out, waved goodbye, and timidly climbed the concrete stairs to my house. I kept looking back because none of the cars pulled off until I was well inside the door.

I knew that Papa would be waiting up for me. In fact, I fully expected a lecture, a smack, or both. I never bothered to prepare my defense because this time, I knew I was wrong. I took advantage and I prepared myself to accept the consequences.

Entering the hall between the outside door and the one leading into the living room, I briefly paused to take a deep breath. Taking hold of the doorknob, I turned it gently, softly pushed open the door, and stepped in. Just as I heard my friends' cars pull away, I saw my father sitting there on the couch in the dark. The only light was one shining in through the window from the street lamp outside.

Hi, Papa. I braced as I spoke in a low repentant voice. *Sorry I'm so late.*

Papa rose from the couch and began walking toward me, stopping close enough to make direct eye contact. He asked me a couple of questions and I gave him the honest answers. Then, it was silent once again. After a long pause he said

Go sleep now. No wake your sista.

That's all? I thought. *Is he going to just let me go?*

I could not believe it. I had given some thought to a number of different things that could potentially happen this night, actually, morning, but this was not one on the list. I said good night, quietly exhaled and quickly, gently made my way to the bedroom.

Perhaps Papa's only concern was that my friends and I had been drinking. His way of ascertaining my condition was to ask me those few questions checking my coherence and getting close enough to smell my breath at the same time. It seemed he was always one step ahead of me, so I tended to carefully consider his responses. Still, it was a nice graduation present. It was the only one I ever remembered.

With his wife gone and as time passed, Papa's life clearly became all about us and his job at Bethlehem Steel. His unconditional love for our mother was not something that I could appreciate while he was alive. There he was, left to raise his children without their mother in the same house; one instead, who went off to work a full time job and establish a new life as a part time visiting mother. It was his perfect opportunity to justify hating her and turn the entire Arabic community and even her children against her. Instead, he often reminded us of her unique relationship to us, fortifying his order to respect her. In his country, she would have been severely punished for such an outrage. In the end, he may not have understood but eventually, he seemed to stop fighting her on it. What followed is a seemingly unending series of ups and downs, with mother making appearances that we children would erroneously interpret as a return. But just like Papa, we never gave up hope.

And perhaps here is where his holding on created an inner conflict that would manifest regularly as his harsh words sometimes failed to be consistent with his actions. Other than yelling back at her sometimes in a gruff manner, he rarely said no when she asked for things. He might have goaded her a bit but in the end, it always seemed like Mom won the battles, if we judge winning by the individual getting what they wanted in the first place. Like with the German Shepherd puppy, when Mom first brought him home from her job in the early 60s. Mom was so well liked by her boss at Cadet Cleaners where she worked as a supervisor, that he offered her to take one of the male pups free for her five children. He told Mom not to say anything to anyone, since he had been selling them for seventy-five dollars each. Mom was surprised, complimented and jumped at the chance to take the beautiful puppy home to us. He was a purebred, she said, had papers and everything. When she first brought him to us, she brought a cardboard box and told us to keep him under the kitchen table while we trained him.

No dok, Papa had said when she arrived. But we were thrilled, of course, with the little brown and black beauty.

Mom was convinced it was a good idea for many reasons.

Saleh, let the kids have the dog. He's a good dog, people pay good money for these puppies, I got it for nothing just for them.

No, Papa said again and again, the dog would have to go back.

It wasn't like we did not have dogs in our home before. Papa often spoke of Beauty, a beloved white Alaskan Husky, who after repeated street mishaps had to be given away. Papa knew someone at Bethlehem who lived on a farm and thought it was better that this energetic runner be placed somewhere he could be free. And then there was Lucky, a German Shepard mix, who after having bitten a couple of people, was taken temporarily to the dog pound and soon after he returned home he was discovered to be blind. It wasn't long before he became ill and died.

While we all took turns during that long first night, responding to the sweet pup's yelps, it was Papa who was discovered caressing him in the morning.

We could keep him, Papa? We cried over and over.

We'll see, he said, and then *Yes, Yes, we keep the dok. What we call him?*

Duke, my sister said, knowing from Mom that his father's name was Duke.

It was the same way whenever we had social events sponsored by the schools. Papa would usually begin with "no," to which we would offer numerous explanations, enlisting Mom's support, which she then took on, and Papa would eventually give in. My sophomore date dance was a touch and go crisis until my girlfriends and I concocted the devious plan that involved writing a letter to my father and forging a nun's signature. Mom assisted greatly in convincing Papa because she would drive the two of us to the event and his Dad would pick us up and take us home, which evidently caused Papa to feel secure enough to allow me to go. When I wanted to go to my prom, there was a need to explain what a prom was first, using careful language because it involved a member of the opposite sex.

Crom? What's crom? He asked, needling me.

*A **Prom**, Papa*! I said exasperatingly and emphasizing the 'P.' And again, Mom to the rescue. I needed her to buy the dress anyway; Papa was never going to consent to that. The idea of his sixteen-year-old daughter going somewhere with a sixteen-year-old boy was I guess, too...well, *American*! We finally won, but it always got so close that I could never be sure it would happen. He kept us all on edge each time there was such an impending event, and with four girls, it happened often enough.

Three Gate at Bethlehem Steel

Somewhere in all of my childhood, there was a consciousness about what my father gave up for us kids, about how his devotion precluded a social life, had he even wanted one. I was always grateful that Papa had "the Plant" because he loved it so much there. The unappealing environment and often harsh conditions were never a deterrent to the workers at Bethlehem Steel. The plant was a safe haven; it was a place for men to be men without excusing themselves. The unmistakable camaraderie added to its allure and the sense of security. Hard labor was something to take pride in, not to fear. And Papa certainly took great pride in his job there.

Bethlehem Steel was more than the place he worked. It literally was Papa's home away from home, the way he felt his worth to himself and to his children. The Plant helped identify his place in this country and in life. It was where he could hone his skill in English among other co-worker immigrants and where he was able to cultivate strong lasting friendships with all kinds of people from a variety of backgrounds. Even once he had to retire, Papa had his children read the Bethlehem newsletter and any other literature that came through the mail. He wanted to keep up with everything, not only what applied to him as a retiree. Because I listened to every detail about where and how Papa worked and the way the 'political' system worked, I did have a good understanding about the industry and that particular facility. Learning even more about the Plant, its working conditions and the individuals who worked there became my pleasure finally, in the end, when I came to the research library in Lackawanna, New York.

For many immigrants like my father, a job in the steel industry allowed them to gain a foothold in the U.S. From just after World War II until the late 1950's, demand for American steel was high enough that our mills could almost name their prices. For the blue-collar steelworker, there was plenty of work and the wages were decent. Papa, like many laborers, was attracted by the pay. In addition to supporting his children, he earned enough that he was often able to send money back home to his family *in the old country.*

Immigrant laborers like my father had a lot in common. They were selfless industrious family men, filled with optimism and willingness. They could not afford to be negative, believed in themselves and that they had the ultimate say in their own success or failure. It was almost as if they knew no better, were too little aware of all that could go wrong. Although their shot at the American dream did more to benefit their children, they were content to earn a good wage for supporting their families and to be able to save money for the future, or God forbid, that *rainy day.*

There was a mystique about the plant, too. It became personified by an embracing American father, creating a sanctuary for those who continued to be challenged by the English language yet wanted the assurance of good wages and great benefits. It provided perhaps a great equalizer with contemporary professionals. It allowed the workers to feel productive and needed, I suppose, contributing members of a team with a greater purpose. Thus it created a kind of dependence among men like my father, but it was also a community where the men watched out for each other, whether they spoke the same language or not.

Papa cultivated good friendships at the Plant, also, counting on them to cover for him in the event of an emergency with his kids, when he might have to leave earlier than at the end of his scheduled shift. In those cases, one of the men would "punch out" for him so he could avoid getting his pay docked. In the reciprocal understanding the men had, he would perform this same service for others when necessary.

Probably the one thing that Papa had not had in common with many, if any, of his fellow workers was being a single father. For Papa, life was consumed with two primary aspects: his children, and the Steel Plant. He took his job very seriously, held a great reverence for the Plant and although it meant more time away from his family, he liked and often accepted offers to work extra hours. The overtime pay was an added security for a proud man concerned with the welfare of five children.

There is no doubt that he could never be sure how long he would be permitted to remain employed. His date of birth had changed often, depending on how old he found he needed to portray himself. Now it would work against him, as he would desire to change the direction of time. I was always convinced that if Papa had his druthers, he would have worked until the day he died.

The steel plant became a melting pot of various groups of immigrants who did not mind the grimy hard labor. Like much of America at that time, it was no secret that the European whites who had the executive positions hired "their own kind" to manage the plants. This often meant that the safer and cleaner jobs went to favored whites, while the dirty, hot, less safe positions were distributed amongst various ethnic groups.

Perhaps it was feelings of vulnerability that impelled the men to quickly catch on to playing by the rules and learning the 'system' at the Plant. Oftentimes, in fact, the laborers were told that if they wanted a better job, they must "take care of their boss," so they developed survival techniques that included what we might call bribery. The men seemed to acccpt this as the way things were done at the plant. As a foreigner in America, one simply did what one had to do.

Papa joked about it with us at the time but I hardly recognized it for the seriousness that it may have been. He used to have my older sister and I pack an extra tuna or egg salad sandwich in his lunch box for various favors, particularly to "rest" a bit on those late and double shift nights. (Sleeping on the job, although not officially permitted, would be tolerated under certain conditions, especially upon completion of assigned work.) This set up also was convenient to Papa when he had to respond to emergency calls from his children while under a babysitter's care.

Record tons of steel was being produced annually at Bethlehem Steel's Lackawanna plant. Three eight hour shifts meant that it was a 24-hour roaring daily operation, lighting up the night skies with its big bellowing orange fire clouds that were visible for miles. The steel plant set on property that bordered on the shores of Lake Erie just south of Buffalo. At one time, hailed as the "Eighth Wonder of the World," Bethlehem was the third largest steel plant in the United States. With an annual payroll of approximately $120million, it employed just over 21,000 people at its peak. The city in which the plant was located, Lackawanna, only had about that number in total population.

Despite the conditions, Papa continued to enjoy his plant. Inside those gates it was a man's world, gruff and profane. He would be assigned to the coke oven, blast furnace and the open hearths. It was said that the Arabs and the Hispanics were chosen for labor exposing them to the greatest amount of heat because *they were accustomed to it.* It was the unions that addressed the ethnic domination apparent in the departments, ultimately resulting in a significant slowdown of scandalous discriminations. In the mean while, however, they were tolerated by the corporation and endured by the workers.

After 1941, the unions had already assisted in ensuring a higher degree of fairness with the institution of a seniority and grievance system, time and a half pay for overtime, and vacation time. Indeed, most needs had been achieved through the union and the laborers were very grateful for that, remaining loyal to the union until the end. For Papa, the plant was responsible for him becoming an inveterate union man and a Democrat, insisting that the "working man" is only served by that particular political affiliation.

Papa became so committed to this that he regularly exercised his right to vote and never missed an election while he could still physically get to a voting booth. As much as he loved his country, he appreciated his American citizenship that granted him the right to vote and directly participate in the outcome of elections. I was well into my twenties when I finally realized that Papa was a straight party line voter. At first, I was appalled by this. Because he was having trouble with his eyesight at the time, he had brought me into the booth with him. Papa knew most of the people up for election, but I began reading the options to him when he interrupted,

Which one Democrat?

Well, this one, I started, *but I will read you…*

Never mind, this line Democrat? He pointed for confirmation.

Yes, Papa, I responded.

Okay, he said, and with that he pulled all the levers on the one side of the booth. I just stood there momentarily startled, with my eyes fixed on the father I just knew understood politics. He pulled back the curtain and looked back at me.

What??? Whassamatta with you, yaa Dolah? I vote Democrat!

Then he let out a laugh at my disbelieving countenance and joked with a few of the ladies on the way out. There was no point in further discussion. I already knew how he felt about being a Democrat, that it was his party of choice as a working man. I closed my mouth and decided that he had a right to express himself any way he chose with his vote.

Working conditions at the plant would remain less than ideal, especially in the departments to which Papa had been assigned. In the coke ovens and blast furnaces, it was an inferno where the air was dirty and the noise ear shattering. It was necessary for the workers to wear hard hats and large goggles. The danger of carbon monoxide was a daily occupational hazard in the blast furnaces. And nothing would prevent the blasts of black dust that filled facial pores in Papa's little face. Sometimes I would get up on his lap to position myself in an attempt to extract them from his cheeks and chin where they often settled, but he rarely sat still for that.

Comon, comon, illa yaa Dolah, he'd say.

I insisted on extracting just a few each time, encouraging him to be patient. Papa's patience was far greater than his vanity and I had to appeal to him where I could win.

The open hearths were not much better. The ethnic men, who were assigned to this department where the steel was melted, required a great deal of stamina to get by. Even with safety equipment, steelworkers were treated for heat exhaustion, exposure to dangerous gases, and serious burns.

Men faced potential peril daily. There were broken bones and loss of hearing suffered by the laborers. At the more extreme end, there had been fatalities. Accidental deaths were attributed to falls from unsafe cranes and scaffolds, or to being crushed. A few men even extinguished in the scalding metal. In 1969, the Lackawanna medical clinic logged 58,956 emergency visits from steelworkers, exceeding the number of emergencies at the largest local hospital in that same year.

Besides his face, Papa's hands bore the signs of hard labor at the plant. Although always soothing to me especially when he'd rub my hurt stomach for long periods, they were rough and hard in spots and also dark with the black dust that refused to wash away. As a child, I thought everyone at the plant worked like and looked like Papa. Naturally, the details of conditions on the job were unknown to me as a child. Papa never mentioned how hard he worked, nor did I understand enough to ask questions. I had not realized there were jobs that involved little or no amount of physical threat nor could I have known of the idea of ethnic stereotypes and how foremen assigned jobs.

Preparing for work at the Plant was a daily ritual. While I was still little enough, I used to sit under the sink peering up at my father while he shaved. I watched quietly as he rinsed the brush in the hot, running water and swished it into the mug of hard soap, creating enough suds to apply foam to his face.

Then came the razor. I anticipated every facial contortion necessary to slide the razor across his face, ridding section by section of coarse whiskers with each gentle, downward stroke. I mimicked through the entire procedure. I knew never to speak during this ritual for fear it would cause my father to nick himself.

He wore long underwear to work all year long. He said that in the summer, it helped to protect him against the heat from the furnaces. In the winter, it naturally protected against the cold. Because his calves were so thin, he was able to wrap his thermal underwear bottoms around each ankle before inserting his foot into high rubber boots.

And there was the unmistakable residual plant smell to the clothes Papa wore to work. Washing failed to remove the smell of fire and steel but I liked it. It represented stability to me. If Papa loved working there, I had always assumed that it was for far greater reason than providing us with a living and I trusted Papa's judgment.

"Swing shift" at the steel plant oftentimes meant that Papa left home in the later evening like 9:30 PM to make it to work by 10:30—10:45PM for the 11:00 to 7:00 a.m. shift. His availability the entire next day made it well worth the sacrifice to not have him home while we slept. He usually made it back in time to say goodbye to us in the morning, had lunch for us as we returned home to eat, and made supper so that we could eat together once we were all home for the day. He frequently met us after school for the better-than one-mile walk home. That was something to look forward to, since the bullies never bothered us while Papa was around.

Our father was the little man who carried a big stick. Literally. It was known around the neighborhood and amongst our school friends, especially to the kids who bothered us, that Mr. Saleh often met his children when they came home for lunch or returned home at the end of the day. Sometimes, when the particular shift permitted, he would be there both times of the day. And on these days, these times, Papa carried a walking stick, not to scare anyone, just because he liked it. The children joked about it and even made us feel more odd than we already did, but we still looked forward to it. And for me, I felt protected.

Papa did not drive himself to work nor did he ever drive or get driven to pick us up from school. *Walking good exercise*, he said. Although he knew how to drive, he maintained an official license for only a brief period. I actually never remembered my father at the wheel of a car. The only reason I even know that he once held a license was because one day I found a renewal stub that was to have been issued on September 30, 1956. He was likely apprehensive about passing some aspect of the driver test, but he never mentioned it. Whenever he was approached about why he did not drive, however, he appeared very nonchalant and asked rhetorically: *For what*?

To get to the Plant, therefore, he was forced to either arrange for or hitch a ride. Papa usually operated somewhere between his two options, probably to cover himself. He would await his prearranged ride on the busy intersection a couple of blocks from our home, keeping his thumb out for passing cars all the while. Papa was good at contingency plans because he rarely depended on anyone and never expected too much. *You never be sure*, he'd say. *Just in case…*

Once when he was waiting for his plant buddy, a black man named Whitey, to come by at the corner of Michigan and Myrtle Avenue, Papa was approached by two or three young thugs. They asked for money. In my father's inimitable way, he outright refused, probably unable to resist offering a mini lecture on self-reliance. Before very long, a couple of others presented themselves from behind some bushes and the gang attacked. In the scuffle, one of the men got hold of an empty whiskey bottle, and used it to hit Papa over the head. The blood was evidently enough to scare them away, so they never did get any money. Soon after, my father's ride arrived and when he caught sight of what had happened, Whitey insisted on taking Papa to the hospital. They had together managed to place something on the open wound to stop the blood flow and got into the car. All the while, Papa protested, saying, *I'm alright, just take me to work.*

In general, Papa, like many of his countrymen who came to America, was moved by a fearless desire to provide for his family and make a good, decent living. But there were times when it seemed Papa feared so little, it was dangerous and foolish. That is why it is easier for me to think that he was only confident and courageous. It is quite possible, however, that he acted from sheer terror at times. But from the looks of it, when the 'fight or flight' response kicked in, Papa always chose to fight.

Maintaining a brave posture was indigenous to Papa's background; courage and bravery are critical factors in maintaining one's self-esteem. He would never wear fear on his face. Perhaps naiveté played a role, when ignorance is true bliss. Nonetheless, it did not always work in keeping him safe from harm.

The head wound required several stitches to close. When I first heard the news I got an immediate nosebleed, something that happened to me often as a child. I had to lie on the bed for a very long time, using a cloth to firmly pinch my nose. And when I heard the entire story, I could not comprehend my father's reaction. I wondered if he had spoken out of delirium or if he had no idea as to the extent of his injury. I even considered that he may have been insecure about his position at the Steel Plant, not wanting to ever take time off. Answers never come but I know one thing. It seemed to me that Papa was one of the toughest guys on this earth.

Within the plant, it was not uncommon to hear the men refer to one another by their ethnic background, but it was not necessarily in a pejorative sense as we might think of it today. They'd distinguish one another by "the Italian guy," "the Irishman." Papa called anyone of Hispanic origin "South America," and said that his particular bosses were mainly "Bolacks" (Polish men). Some workers poked fun at the Arabs with their long, odd names and funny religion. (A number of the more devout Muslims would be observed taking time to stop, face east to Mecca, and kneel down to pray five times daily.) Since formal introductions were rarely made in the departments and most people had difficulty with pronunciation of Arabic names, the men would often make one up, Americanizing their actual name or simply resorting to "Ali," one of the more common and easily pronounceable Arabic names.

But the "foreigners" were a whole lot less naive than they were often taken for. If their bosses or supervisors were speaking English and laughing at them, it is sure that the men were cajoling and laughing all along with or at them in their own native languages. Still, they did manage to coexist in peace at the Plant. All survived the formation of the United Steel Workers Union, which Papa came to revere, in 1941. It was said that the net effect of the union was to break down ethnic boundaries as it put an end to the favoritism and the tremendous informal power of the foremen.

Despite his efforts to stay on as long as he could, Papa was forced into retirement. The company was as confused about his age as he probably was (one became eligible for 100% of his pension at age 62) when he reluctantly left in about 1970. By that time, overtime hours were a thing of the past and Bethlehem Steel was slowly dying its painful death in the area.

In the years following his retirement, Papa continued to enjoy being able to discuss the company news with some friends who had remained employed there. He wanted to keep up with what was going on in the world of the steel industry, especially with the Lackawanna plant. I suspect he had kept informed for personal reasons as well, to ensure that his benefits would not be negatively affected as the situation grew more bleak.

As it turned out, Papa left at the right time. The schedule of his retirement coincided with the downfall of the Lackawanna plant and ultimately of the domestic steel industry. What had begun as a business with an indisputable captive market was slowly giving way to a dwindling demand for American steel. Imports were capturing a greater and greater percentage of the business. High and increasing environmental cost considerations had swiftly become a significant factor; imposed government regulations included onerous pollution requirements. With a smaller share of the market, profitability was low, and major layoffs had begun.

The 1970's had become unsettled times for the entire industry and the Lackawanna plant, already down to about half its peak operation level, had been contributing to the industry demise in a personal way. For some time, it had been considered a problem in labor relations (the first Civil Rights case in the area involved an employee of Bethlehem Steel's Lackawanna plant), creating more trouble than all other plants combined. It was believed that the local town taxes were anywhere from two to five times greater in Lackawanna than in any other Bethlehem plant. Management had thought for some time that the town had been exploiting the plant with exorbitant taxes.

But the town had underestimated the impact of such alleged practice, maintaining that the plant was too great an investment to Bethlehem. In 1977, with increasing sentiment from headquarters to shut down, employment at the Lackawanna plant dropped from 11,500 to 8,000.

Three generations of families in Lackawanna had been employed by the plant since 1900, a great many of them being immigrants. By 1920, foreigners had accounted for approximately 82% of the town's population, many of whom were Arabs.

As Papa's fellow steelworkers became unemployed, they quickly realized that they might never return to a job in steel. Adding to the already dark picture were local perceptions that would ultimately damage the reputation of the individual worker. In an effort to assist in job searches, the company sent word out to potential employers. But area employers hesitated to hire the steelworkers. They claimed that the unions had spoiled these men; that they wanted high wages, excellent benefits and were essentially lazy.

The situation gave way to finger pointing. The union would claim that the company was top heavy in management and that there was some sort of corporate vendetta against Lackawanna. Company managers had pointed to unrealistic environmental regulations, declining productivity and local taxes. The workers would find fault in changing car-manufacturing requirements. The bottom line, sad as it was, is that all parties and all facets contributed to the plant's decline; no one was planning ahead. Papa's beloved Bethlehem was essentially self-destructing.

Those who were on the outside looking in blamed the unions for the layoffs and shutdowns. They thought that union demands had been too great, that American steel had been non-competitively priced due to the unreasonably high cost of labor. The fact was, however, that union demands in terms of rate of pay did not drain the company. (Wages had not exceeded 40% of sales since the 1940's). What contributed more to the financial strain had more to do with union-dictated work practices, such as featherbedding, requiring an employer to hire or retain more workers than needed.

By 1977, substantial losses made it clear that there would be an eventual plant shutdown. No longer the vital, growing organization that it once was, it was now running a minimal operation with a small fraction of total capacity. In 1981, foreign steel market penetration in America climbed from 14% to 25% in one quick year.

The following year, 1982, was the toughest one yet. By year-end, on December 27, 1982, Bethlehem Steel made the long-anticipated announcement: all steel making would be terminated in 1983. The partial shutdowns over the past 13 years easily predicted the ultimate outcome precluding shock but not he pain, which endured for some time.

On October 1, 1983, all operations ceased in the one-industry town of Lackawanna. Only about 1100 of the remaining 7300 employees would qualify for pensions. The exit of these men and women walking out of the gates for the last time would be characterized as a devastating silence.

In researching the Bethlehem Steel story in the Lackawanna library, I came across a piece of memorabilia that brought tears to my eyes. It was a sign:

NOTICE
No. 3 Gate Will Be Closed Permanently
Effective 19, Dec. '82
No access to or exit from the plant allowed

Flashbacks raced through my mind. That was Papa's gate; the one from which we so often picked him up. It had closed forever only 18 days after he died.

Discipline in Chaotic Times

There are times I still wonder how Papa made it through the pre-adolescent and adolescent years of five children going it alone. Juggling all the balls he had to in the tumultuous times of the mid-to-late 60's had to be more than he bargained for. I was still in grade school when the country mourned the death of a beloved President, John F. Kennedy. Soon after, racial riots had begun down South and were threatening to spread north. A brief four years later, I was in high school when America found itself unwittingly drawn further and further into war in Vietnam. Young men who refused to participate in the draft were resorting to drastic measures to voice their rejection. I came to personally know older boys who anxiously held their breath waiting for their draft number to be called. It would not be long before deferments were no longer being made available. If you were of age, you faced the real possibility of going to fight in a war that fewer and fewer Americans supported. Frightened and angry, college students vehemently protested with public demonstrations that sometimes ended in violence.

Meanwhile, all eyes temporarily turned to the plight of discrimination. Racial riots persisted; blacks pressured for and demanded their civil rights. Just as millions of other Americans, my family helplessly viewed all the action on television. Then, the country was once again jolted with the murder of Martin Luther King. Two months later, Robert Kennedy was assassinated as he campaigned for the Presidency in Los Angeles. It appeared that the country was close to anarchy. And with the protracted war in Vietnam now raging out of control, people had grown weary. Public demonstrations continued in protest; by this time there were half a million American soldiers in Vietnam.

The youth of the 50's and 60's had become a force to be reckoned with. They asked a lot of questions and were not satisfied with the answers from those in authority. Adding insult to injury, it was a time when the threat of nuclear war loomed heavily. It was easy to grow cynical about the government. No one could be trusted. Feeling hopeless and helpless, we were a disillusioned lot and set out to proclaim this in every way that we could. The "Me-Generation" became inevitable.

It was around this same time that Papa was feeling his own personal sadness and oppression as the supervising members at Bethlehem urged him toward retirement. While some people anticipate the termination of their work life with a great deal of positive excitement and look forward to doing all the things they were unable to do because of a lack of time, there are others who would much rather work up until some physical limitation prevents them from so doing. These people perceive retiring to be a precursor to death. Unfortunately, Papa was of this latter type. It appeared as if he aged overnight in an effort to look the part.

I suppose that it was fortunate for my father that my brother and I were the only two who presented challenges that demanded his close attentions. With the five of us ranging from about eleven to eighteen years of age by this time, there were the typical individual dramas going on, most of which he had to acknowledge. I know that Papa pleaded his case for continuing his employment and even bought some additional time with the steel plant, but the personal traumas he endured were mostly kept private. Papa would suffer in silence.

It sounds odd to even admit this, but it turns out that it was best we were unaware of what was happening to our father and how negatively he had been affected by his forced retirement. Inasmuch as I understand the need for parents to share and to be open with their children, there is value in parents demonstrating self-control. It could have been threatening to us; we could have been even more frightened than we already were. When I eventually understood the impact of Papa's loss, I realized how strong he had to be and the restraint he had to have had not to express himself in some way.

Probably one of his greatest coping tactics was the discipline he exacted on his family. In the traditional custom of his country, Papa was an exceedingly strict, authoritarian father. We learned quickly that the other kids can do it argument was never going anywhere with Papa. He just did not nor would he ever concern himself with what other children were permitted to do. His voice was firm.

I don't care what they (other kids) do—not my children!

Besides making decisions about whom we would befriend and what type of clothing we were allowed to wear, there were consequences to unacceptable behavior. Usually, those consequences would involve some type of corporal punishment. There were no surprises and it was consistent. We always knew that if we disobeyed, we would pay. And, he was relentless about it, too. There was one night when Delilah and I locked ourselves in the bathroom, hoping to escape Papa's brown leather belt by outlasting his endurance. After about the third hour, I remember peeking through the keyhole and seeing him still sitting there hunched over with both elbows on his knees holding onto his worn brown leather belt. We were so tired, and it was a school night, after all. At some point, we had decided to take our beating like big girls and get to bed. As we ran out of the bathroom, we tried apologizing and begging Papa's forgiveness. He only gave us one quick whip each.

My three younger siblings had their turn in the bathroom, too. As my youngest sister, Sinia, recalls, He just needed to make his point. It was just one smack, usually a light tap with the belt, and it was over. A reminder of who was boss. Sinia also remembers many a night when our brother Eddie would get locked out of the house for disobeying or coming home too late, and she would let him in through a window after Papa had retired to another room out of sight. I personally think Papa counted on that. And when Delilah came home after her curfew when she was 19, she spent the night sitting up on the back upstairs porch. It was shortly after that when Delilah decided it was time to move out. She and Papa did not speak for an entire year, even though Papa always asked about her a million different ways the entire time.

It was possible to completely avoid that belt, however, even if he had outlasted us in the bathroom. We learned fairly early that a fake cry here and there may succeed in eliciting Papa's sympathy for the moment. The funny thing was that the tap hardly hurt, it was more the sight of that notorious belt that rarely failed to strike fear in our hearts. Then again, that may have been his objective.

The belt was not Papa's exclusive disciplinary tool. Sometimes in a fit of frustration, when he called you every one of your sisters and even brother's name only to finally arrive at yours, he might throw a slipper or lightly grab a handful of your hair into his large hand. And sometimes he could be very effective with no action and very few words.

The first time I became engaged I was only nineteen years old. Actually, it was a secret engagement. The only people who knew besides me was the man I was engaged to and some of his friends. Papa and I argued about Michael but the tension did seem to let up after a couple of years. I was at least able to invite the gentleman into my home and had begun dating him openly. One day during our secret engagement, my father was sitting by quietly while I spoke to my boyfriend on the phone. After I hung up, I sat down on the sofa in the living room, near to where Papa was sitting. While I could see him thinking, I silently questioned the precise content of those thoughts. But after we sat there in some degree of uncomfortable silence for what seemed an eternity, he turned to me and said, *You will work for him.*

Excuse Me? I said with my face. No words, pure ambivalence—wanting to know and not wanting to. If I just stay silent, there will be no discussion.

He repeated, *You will work for that man.*

I was caught too off-guard to respond and Papa left the room in a rather somber carriage.

I have thought of that moment often enough to suspect that my father possessed a wisdom that one could not deny. I never married Michael but I did come to understand Papa's expression of concern. While every father wishes for his daughter to marry a good and decent man, he is also likely mindful of the man's ability to financially support his daughter and a family. Practical aspects of financial security did not escape my father anymore than it likely does any other parent wishing the best for his or her child.

For some long period after this event, my boyfriend, while one of the most intelligent men I have had the pleasure to know and love, had not settled into gainful employment. And it was he who was to break our engagement in the end with a line that validated Papa's prophecy. He had explained how I wanted too much of life and how he simply did not intend to set the world on fire. It was as though he and Papa knew me better than I did myself at the time.

When I met my second real American boyfriend I was only 17 years old, the July after I had graduated from high school. Michael was a musician and I was illegally in the establishment with my friends where he was playing in a band, *The National Trust*. Michael was six years older than I was and an amazing self-taught musician. I fell so in love with him that I could not imagine hiding him from Papa for very long.

At first, I had lied to Michael and told him that I was 19 (I had been carrying my older sister's birth certificate in case I was caught) but soon after when I revealed my real age, all he said was *Don't let any one know, especially my friends*. He liked my innocence but was certain that he would be teased mercilessly, especially when he was being sought after by all the "cool" girls, most of whom were a bit older and definitely wiser.

It was not long before I brought him to meet Papa but it was no easier even as I was now almost an independent adult, with a job and the beginning of my college life. Michael tried hard for Papa to like him, but there were conversations and episodes of us bickering that Papa heard and saw and he let us know it. There were starts and stops. To tell the truth, I really think that Papa could not help but like this friendly blonde hair blue-eyed scrapper who easily called him Papa as did his children and some close friends. Still, even as there were days when my father seemed really okay with Michael, I could not bring myself to admit that I was so madly in love that I would have married him in a heartbeat. So, we pledged our love to a small group of friends one night at a local Italian restaurant, the Roseland, and began our secret engagement. We would wait until we completed our education, we would not let on, even though Michael gave me a small diamond ring that I cherished until the diamond fell out, likely a victim of being pulled on and off my finger in an effort to maintain the ruse.

Our true love never ran smooth, though. We broke up and got back together so many times I stopped counting. At one point I remember thinking that we will never work but I will love him forever and I do. The funny thing is that when I see him today, which is very rare because he lives thousands of miles away in the west, one of our most enjoyable subjects is still Papa. Michael still says that he was a cool guy and takes great pleasure in reminiscing about our cherished moments with my dear father.

For the remainder of my dating years, Papa did not meddle a great deal further. Like most parents do, I believe he had an influence in whom all his children selected as life partners anyway. In a sort of passively aggressive way, it was clear that the person, American though he/she may necessarily be, had to be a good person.

I continued to have dates and even occasional boyfriends here and there throughout college life and beyond, but Papa rarely met them. In Arabic custom, dating is not exactly expected or accepted for long periods, neither is dating a variety of people casually. So I dated them while living away on campus (even as the college was local) and in an apartment for a short period and while away in Europe when I studied in Spain. But the very next man that Papa became aware of and with whom I spent a great deal of time, Papa insisted, *You ar luf? Then, you marry*. And so I did.

Actually, my brother and I were the first to marry and therefore the only two who Papa lived long enough to see married. Papa got to see my brother's two eldest children, two boys, thankfully, and that was a wonderful thing. Delilah remains single and Minnie and Sinia both married men they had been dating when Papa passed away. They had not been as active as I was in the dating scene and I think both felt they had Papa's blessings. Between them they had five children—adding to Ed's five—all people in whom Papa surely takes great pride.

Rebellion and Heartache

Undeniably, I spent most of my youth feeling sorry for myself. Sorry that I did not have two parents at home and sorry that the parent I lived with did not live as other Americans did. Some of my most frustrating experiences were the times I spent attempting to explain what to other (American-born) parents was normal, everyday kids stuff. Most of my arguments that used that rationale meant nothing to Papa. He could not be dissuaded from his values and therefore was resolute in his decision-making. So that even with my feelings of deprivation, I could not help but accept what was unchangeable.

And just because he was neither young nor American-born nor familiar with what American children were expected to do, it wasn't like Papa was easily fooled. Admittedly, I spent my youth being the most likely to be a problem as I took every opportunity to push as far as I would be allowed to go, practically anything I thought I could get away with. Often Papa would let me know and sometimes he'd just let me go, but he always knew. With a mere look, Papa could make me feel transparent. It never ceased to amaze me how well he was able to walk that fine line between giving enough rope and knowing when to pull it in to be able to successfully keep five people in control and out of trouble.

I did tend to complain about being different and about what I considered to be Papa's harsh rules and disciplinary tactics that seemed to stem from his cultural background but the truth is that there were good things about being first generation American. Besides having a direct connection to my heritage, I experienced the inextricable link between my father's religion and culture. This made it easy to follow and comprehend; it is black and white. There is hardly a trace of gray, little, if any, ambiguity. Even if we maintain a philosophical difference such as blatant female subjugation in the culture, for example, we could see the benefits of reliable dogma. There is no skirting of issues. It simply is what it is. My thinking may been influenced by my life experience, the uncertainty I felt due to not living in an intact familial situation, which made me appreciate the idea of an either/or conviction. And while some punishments common in Papa's Arabic culture could be considered Draconian, being made clearly aware of consequences meant that I always knew where I stood.

Islam is essentially a way of life with rules made not to be broken. While in a homogeneous society this is easily accomplished, for me and my sisters and brother there were times when it was difficult to remember that we were Americans living in America.

Once my arguments had passed, however, I did find a way to honor my father's wishes. What made it worse was that my older sister and my two younger ones tended to remain consistently obedient to Papa's every command. When I did go against his advice, Papa used to say things like *You'll see*. I hated that, because he was usually so right on. I would "see" and many times I could not admit to him that he had been right. He once warned me that I might be the daughter most like my mother. I guess that was a bad thing because as much as he loved her, he did not approve of her behavior either.

I did not want to be like my mother but I was never clear about why that was. I mean, there was the obvious issue of her choice to leave her family, but I was so confused I don't believe I quite knew what to feel about that—or perhaps I blocked out those feelings. I never hated my mother because she left. I did not like that she was gone when it came to family type affairs or when it was inconvenient, like for a quick response to a teacher or something. As far as I was concerned, all my basic needs were being met and I did feel mom loved us and cared about us because her contact was unfailing. It was she, not

Papa, who came to the rescue about stylish clothing, an imperative when you're young and growing up. If I faulted her for anything, it was for a sadness I perceived in my father and that was one heavy toll I likely paid. I felt responsible.

Perhaps my challenging temperament was nothing more than what most referred to as my adventurous nature, just like mom once was. Even with regret of this unattractive distinction for many years, I accept its truth. My brother gave Papa a separate set of headaches. But then, Arabs have a different set of rules for sons and daughters, so there is no sense comparing between the sexes. The worst to happen in one of my fights with my father was the time I blurted out: I hate you! Which he unfortunately remained committed to reminding me of for the rest of his healthy life.

Nice, you say that to your father,

He had said—or asked—at the time, with penetrating sad eyes that made me want to immediately take it all back and swear to God that I was only joking. But it was too late. He was hurt and I was the big jerk of a teenage daughter who could neither control her emotions nor be big enough to apologize and therefore was bound to building serious regrets.

Remember when you say that to me—'I hit you'?

He would ask me later.

Yes, Papa, I remember, and I am so very sorry.

Perhaps it is with some degree of irony that I was the first of Papa's daughters to marry and the only one he actually saw get married. In fact, after enduring the third degree, which I fully expected and warned my American fiancée about, we decided that we would comply with Papa's request to have an Imam (Islamic representative) perform a type of no-frills ceremony at Papa's house two days before my Catholic wedding. We sat on the floor as Jack was directed to repeat a number of sentences in Arabic, initiated by the Imam, while Papa and I listened. Then the Imam and Papa spoke in Arabic, a number of times back and forth. At the end, Jack looked relieved and understandably puzzled.

Do you feel married? I asked as we left that day.

No.

Neither do I, I said, and that was it. Although Papa did not come into the Catholic Church the day I was married, he met us back at the hall for the reception. I am grateful that I decided, too, to celebrate the day in both American and Arabic custom, because it made him so happy. I had both an American and Arabic band and there were probably as many Arabs invited as there were Americans and perhaps even more that just decided to show up. We had a great time, with the Americans loving the belly dancer, who approached the patriarch and brought him up onto the dance floor.

We danced the Debke and the bunny hop, listened to rock and roll and the oud, the Middle Eastern lute, all of which my entertainment-loving father absolutely delighted in.

The Company We Keep

Not unlike many parents, Papa vehemently upheld the belief that we are the company we keep. He said that others judge us by our friends, whom we choose reveals how we think of ourselves. More dramatically, he used examples of failed "friendships" to demonstrate the importance of caution. The family, he said, created the nucleus of our most loyal supporters and confidants. He took many opportunities to emphasize that blood is thicker than water and how ultimately, the individual is his own best friend, reinforcing the concepts of accountability and self-reliance. We were to choose individuals who possessed similar values and those who could have a positive influence in our lives. This undoubtedly would have happened naturally as we tend to gravitate toward our own comfort levels, but this was Papa's refusal to remain passive, his preference for not leaving things up to chance. At the same time, it became important to avoid those from whom we could learn nothing, and whose behavior may lead to illegal, immoral or unwise ends.

Because of his strong feelings on this issue, Papa often attempted to choose our friends for us, however impractical it may have been. I believe that I may have suffered the brunt of his standards here. There was a large Polish family, the Kozlowskis, who lived across the street from us with whom Papa preferred we not associate. They did not have a father at home and Papa felt that since the children were highly unsupervised, they could possibly be a negative influence.

One of the girls in this family, Paulette, about my age, did not like me for whatever reason. Perhaps she was aware of how Papa felt and put the word out in the neighborhood was that she was *after me*. My mere presence seemed to bother her and she grabbed every opportunity she could to annoy and terrorize me with ridiculous accusations. Every morning for quite some time, she would watch for me to leave and depending upon who was around at the time, would periodically shove me, challenging me to fight back all the way to school. On most days, I refused to stay after class ended because I knew she would be out there waiting for me once again for the return trip home. Instead, I used to be one of the first kids out of the building and practically run all the way home before she was let out. I was no match for the street-wise public schooler. I hated fighting, reserving that activity for my siblings, and that was usually only verbal warfare. There were even days that I actually talked my father into allowing me to stay home because of Paulette's threats. Of course, this only occurred on the days when his work shift precluded him from walking me to and from school and when I had been particularly concerned because of something that had taken place just prior.

Papa never disclosed the real reasons for my absences to the nuns at my school, preserving my dignity. They would only have shrugged my problem off as innocent childhood shenanigans but I knew better. They didn't have to confront Paulette.

Eventually, I had to face my nemesis, lest she control my very existence. At first, I attempted to talk it out with her in my backyard. I was in the yard; she was on the other side of the fence (I was taking no chances). That strategy failed miserably. The only effect it seemed to have was to make her angrier. She felt compelled to taunt me and dared me to face her without my dog or father or protective older sister.

Then, while Papa was at work one day, I reluctantly agreed to fight her—on the same side of the fence this time. I was prepared to be seriously injured and live with it. Anything to end the drama. But just as we were about to begin, an adult in the neighborhood intervened and she lost her chance, in her words, to *beat the hell out of me*. Now I knew I had better find some other way out of this, or prepare to stay indoors for the rest of my elementary school days. I had lost my nerve and the neighbor siding with me had exacerbated Paulette's reprisal. Then, I thought of the perfect plan.

Everyone including Papa knew that her sister Marsha was a very nice girl. She did not especially get along with Paulette and had heard, along with everyone else in the neighborhood, about my plight. At the risk of sounding cowardly, I must admit that I decided to make friends with this slightly older sister. Actually, my older sister had already befriended her, and had begun negotiating on my behalf. Once it was clear that Marsha was making regular neighborly visits to our home, the vendetta subsided. Somehow my adversary was okay with the idea that we had accepted a member of her family. I do not think it hurt, either, that Paulette was somewhat afraid of her older sister. Papa was okay with it, too, because having felt badly for me, he had gone as far as he could to put an end to his daughter's misery.

My father and her sister had convinced me that Paulette was envious of me, but I never understood why. I did not hate her, in fact, in a strange sort of way I rather liked her and admired her toughness, wishing I had had some of that audacity. I recall rather maturely considering her different problems that made her sad and mad besides her feeling slighted by my not hanging out with her. But I definitely resented what she did to shatter my sense of safety in the little world outside my home.

Papa may have said things because he did not know another way to explain the unexplainable. I guess jealousy seemed plausible enough, but if I was unable to pinpoint exactly what she was jealous of, it did me no good to have this information. Even if I did know, I probably could not have changed anything to make her feel any different. Believe me, I gave it a lot of thought. And since Paulette had managed to turn some of the neighborhood kids against me, I had all these people who seemed to avoid me and I never understood why. I would not have cared so much if they had left it at that, but they rallied on her behalf, causing me to feel even more like an outsider than I already did. I had figured that a girl with such bravado had likely used fear tactics to gain all this support, but that also failed to console me. Like other children, I just wanted to fit in but it remained Papa's wish to have me be proud of who I was and resilient against attack.

Feeding the Hungry

In time, as we settled in to a new life without mom, there were talks, and walks, serious and not-so-serious moments with Papa. We could always be certain that spending time with him meant we were sure to learn something. One fine summer afternoon, while we were all busy playing with friends in the back and side yards, a ragged-looking man walked up with a sign. It read that he was deaf and mute and that he needed money to eat because he was hungry. We all felt badly for the man and a group of us quickly ran to find Papa. We knew from the look on his face and the few Arabic words he muttered that our father had some reservations about this. Nevertheless, he would be happy to feed the poor fellow. Directing the man to a seat at our picnic table in the yard, Papa proceeded into the house to prepare a meal. Before long, he returned with a large plate of eggs and toast, and placed it down on the table in front of the man, gesturing for him to go ahead and eat:

Bis-mil-lah.

After the man devoured everything on the plate, he bowed his head in thanks to Papa and us children. We were happy to see a starved man eat and that is precisely what we did, we sat and stared at the man the entire time he ate. I worried about how and where he would get his next meal.

As the man walked away with his sign placed once again over his chest, he motioned a wave goodbye and turned to head back down the street. My brother noticed that he had left a little pad and pencil on the bench. Without thinking, he yelled out to the man:

Hey, Mister, you forgot something!

The man turned around.

My eyes grew wide as I quickly turned to look at my father. Everyone awaited Papa's response. But he simply shrugged his shoulders.

It's ok, he assured us. *That's why I only give him to eat. He's hungry. It's ok. I no give him money for drink.*

Years later, we all got a lot of laughs out of that incident, and today I consider its significance.

One of the five pillars of Papa's Islamic religion is zakat,—to give to the poor. It is an obligation -fard -of every Moslem who has the means. I believe that Papa simply accepted the event as an opportunity to fulfill his duty while remaining pleased that his caution prevented him from being totally hoodwinked.

Skating on Faith

Also like most parents, Papa was both teacher and preacher. He was consistently willing to impart his knowledge to anyone who would listen, but as his children, we had no choice. The methods varied and at times were difficult, but they were usually memorable.

One particular day stands out in my memory when he taught me a crucial lesson. It is a one that I had never identified while he was alive, but has become all the more powerful a message to me since his passing.

I was only about eight years old at the time. We were at the Boulevard Mall waiting for my mother, who was shopping nearby, when I spotted an ice skating rink that was temporarily positioned in the center of the complex. There were young adults and children skating round and round this man-made ice rink, while parents and others watched. I looked on too, longingly, with my father at my side.

I do not remember exactly what I said, or even if I had verbalized anything at that exact moment. But before I knew it, my father had paid for skate rental and had me seated while he laced up the skates. All the while, I discreetly protested with expressions of concern about my inability to skate, and how *I just know I will fall*... and *I am so afraid*... and... *I just can't!!*..._

But I had great faith in my father. If he was so certain that I could skate, who was I to question? Perhaps he knew something I could not yet understand at this tender age.

Rising to a vertical position in those ice skates scared me half to death. Papa must have seen the terror in my eyes, because he leaned in toward the rink and spoke in a comforting voice:

I stay right here, he said reassuringly.

I got up, hung onto the railing for the first few times around, and then finally let go. I can remember thinking about what Papa had said.:

They (other children can) *do it, you do it, too*! It sounded right, so simple, just like Papa always made things sound. I also knew he would never risk danger to me. Those comforting thoughts strengthened my resolve.

And then, after witnessing my first non-stop trip around the entire rink, Papa smiled back at me. *What I tell you*? He said with every bit of confidence.

I have often recalled this empowering message to myself: we can do anything we want to do so we can expect the best of and for ourselves. So simple yet profound. I also came away with a sense of not being too quick to set limitations. We can predispose ourselves to failure due to irrational made-up fears. That day I learned that most times, "can't" is a euphemism for "won't." That there is power in true conviction: That just like Henry Ford once said, *If you think you can do a thing or think you can't do a thing, you're right.*

Fitting In

Once, just after I had entered my freshman year in the all-girls Catholic high school, I became frustrated with the little "cliques" I saw forming and chose to lash out at my father. After all, I expect I had felt that he was responsible for the way I looked and the name I had, and certainly for the experiences, or lack thereof, I had garnered along the way. I was smart, but certainly not cool, and as far as fashion and makeup were concerned, I had and wore none. It was displaced aggression, of course, as it did not start out as an open discussion about my uniqueness. It was supposed to be about the "cliques," and somewhere along the line I had talked myself into feelings of alienation because of who I was.

I could see the sadness in my father's eyes as I continued to berate his culture saying that everyone at school has lighter skin and "normal" names and goes skiing with their whole family on weekends. But that did not stop me. I hated my stupid, coarse, thick hair and I was embarrassed that I had never been to a slumber party or skied or even wore jeans as they were prohibited due to the zippers being located in the front of the pant. (We could wear slacks with zippers on the side only).

Upon finishing my tirade, I immediately felt bad. The silence that followed was uncomfortable, but it would still be some time when I could get out of my own way to apologize. I was always saying stupid things when I was a teenager, and I was as stubborn as one could be. Papa just walked away. He said nothing just then.

Later, he addressed the issue of self-pride. He told me a few "old country" stories, talked about the value of my uniqueness. He reminded me how people admire my skin and its color, would love to have it and that was why they had to spend hours in the sun when I had it naturally. The same with my hair, he said, telling me of the money women spend on perms to achieve the look that I have with all my big curly hair. He told me that our Arabic names made people remember us and that it was becoming increasingly popular to have names that are not "common," like my friends, Cathy and Suzie. No apologies for the strict discipline; it is necessary, Papa said. It was the only way to teach us and *I could ask the sista, she know*.

A part of me had already begun to accept all that by this time—even if it had to mean that I would not get to wear jeans with front zippers until I was in college. In time, I realized that what I had mistaken for a desire to look like everyone else was actually my need to be accepted despite my differences. Another lesson that Papa helped me understand. Another reason to feel bad for speaking so harshly to someone who loved me and always had the best of intentions.

Papa had a penetrating way of looking at a person that made you feel temporarily insane during the heat of a moment. Maybe it was those deep-set cloudy eyes. That's how I remember that day. His leaving was a way of delaying a talk with me until my sanity was restored. He would not respond until both of us had had an opportunity to reflect on what I had said. The silence was a statement; he would allow me time for my anger to dissipate and would not be lured into an argument with an unreasonable child.

No Grudges

When someone wronged Papa, he dealt with it in that moment and went on. Interesting, but other than reminding us children on occasion of our offenses, he never held grudges. When another countryman housed my mom after she left us, he was at first angry with him, had his words to say, which he did to his face, then seemed to let it go because they were soon on speaking terms. When my Mom met Stanley, the man she has been with for over twenty-five years now, Papa asked his questions, joked about him being a "bollack," and subsequently spoke to and even liked Stanley.

Mom recently told me a story that illustrated Papa's position with her and although I am sure she does not even know this, it brought me to tears when I heard it. Sometime years after she left, perhaps eight or more years later, she was in transition, moving from one apartment to another. Since she needed a place to stay, Papa told her that she could sleep with one of my sisters for the night. Evidently, she retired early, after thanking my father for his offer. About an hour or so later, Papa came in to the bedroom to check on everyone as he always did, and heard Mom having a nightmare. When he discovered that she was not well, he quietly awoke her, standing at her bedside with a glass of water and two aspirin. He had apparently touched her forehead and realized she had had a fever.

You're on fire, he'd explained. *Here, take this*. After she swallowed the aspirin, he said, *Go back sleep now*, and left the room. Mom said she had never forgotten Papa's kindness that night.

But it would appear that my parents' basic feelings toward one another were reciprocal. Living apart from her family, mom had made a habit of coming back and forth *to check up on us kids and really,* she said, *on Saleh, as well.* One morning after we had all gone to school, she was making her check, walking over toward the house and noticed that the front door was unlocked. She looked in through the window and saw Papa lying on the couch. He didn't look well. Mom pushed the door open and called out.

Saleh?

Papa groaned.

Saleh, what's the matter?

I'm sick. Papa did not talk like this unless it was really serious.

Mom walked over and touched his forehead. He was hot, she remembered, very hot.

I'm going to call the doctor, okay?

Papa groaned again.

After mom placed a phone call to Dr. O'Brian, she walked back from the kitchen wall phone to tell Papa that an ambulance was coming. He was going to the hospital. Papa hated hospitals and would routinely reject the notion of having to resort to that level of assistance. But he didn't argue this time. When the ambulance arrived, Mom asked if she could go with them, they said yes and off they went. Mom called in to work to tell them that she would be late.

They also somehow managed to work together when it came to us kids, too, particularly during emergencies. On this occasion mom stopped by on her way home from work at the Cleaners. When she arrived, Papa and my younger sister were sitting on the steps with Minnie sobbing in obvious distress. Papa explained to mom who was growing with anxiety at the sight, that Mena had fallen while trying to skate. Mom placed her in the car immediately and took her to Children's Hospital, soon discovering that Minnie had sprained her leg. When Mom delivered my sister in a cast to school the next day, she spoke to the lovely Mrs. Marconi, Minnie's grade school teacher, and she allayed mom's fears by assuring her that she will take special care of her daughter.

When there were slipups, they were fairly grave. Although mom tended to take care of things that Papa either could not or would not, there were times she still missed things. One of these things was Minnie's eyesight. Then one day when the pastor of St.Columba came to call on mom, he told her that Minnie could not see the black board. They had assigned her a seat up in the front of the classroom, but she was still having difficulty and probably needed to see an eye doctor. *How long had this been going on*, Mom asked and doesn't recall the response, only that she did remember that Minnie had a bad habit of sitting up very close to the television, a practice she vociferously warned against. When she did take her to visit the ophthalmologist, Minnie was immediately given a prescription for pretty serious eyeglasses.

And mom missed something else from this experience. Something that would end up in a discomfiting situation with her boss at Markel. The bill from Minnie's eye doctor came to Myrtle Avenue but it came in mom's name, which unfortunately caused Papa to put it aside and then forget to mention it. After enough weeks passed, the bill went into a collections mode where mom's company was notified and a request for garnishee of her wages was strongly advised. She was surprised and a bit rattled and felt the need to explain but she quietly submitted. She received no paycheck that week.

Papa and the People

Perhaps it was Papa's blue-collar mentality that caused him to appear stronger and tougher than most of my friends' fathers, who had office or sales jobs. I always figured that my father's history lent itself to the evolvement of a thick skin, as one who had grown accustomed to fending for himself and his children in sometimes difficult circumstances. Almost in compliment to his protective posture, there was often a gruffness to his tone. I used to warn my friends that my father meant no harm by the tone and pitch of his voice and his twenty questions about *where you come from? and who is your father and mother?*

To Arabs, the raising of the voice demonstrates strength of emotion with what is being said. This can be a good or bad feeling, but it is nothing personal toward the one being addressed. Besides, Papa's questioning tactic had a hidden agenda. It was just another vehicle for him to assist in our selection of friends. He always believed that the parents and the child were reflections of one another.

It wasn't so much that he cared what your father did for a living; he wasn't asking about status or monetary comfort. Papa wanted to know who your parents were, what they believed in, about their family background, how they were raised. That told him all he needed to know. When my mother spoke of people who "had money" and were "educated," an awfully big deal to mom, he never engaged her in conversation. It hung in the air. There was just no where to go with it, unlike things that actually mattered to him. When it came to people, they were all simply people, no one superior and other than certain unacceptable behaviors, no one inferior. Papa always seemed content, comfortable, and quietly proud of who he was, however humble, always respecting race, religious and nationality differences. Coming from a homogeneous society, I imagine one could be surprised that Papa could remain so neutral, but I think he simply felt that these aspects of an individual were not the determining factor in whether or not they were good people. All were welcome in our home and we never heard any pejorative references in the name of these differences.

Papa had a fairly close black friend whom we regularly traveled by bus to visit. Mr. Johnson and his wife were sweet people who had a nice daughter that babysat for us on occasion. Alexenia became one of our favorite sitters. My father also maintained long-term business relationships with those Jewish owners of furniture, appliances and jewelry—Mr. Zolte, and Maisel and Mr. Howard. He would often tease these gentlemen, but they called each other "cousin," and the associations were bona fide positive ones. Another favorite sitter was "Tata," an Hispanic woman and single mother with one son who played with my brother, an important detail to a boy who was stuck with four sisters.

All kinds of people were invited and came to our home. They were all colors, all religions and all walks of life. Papa was actually the one who introduced me to the concept of homosexuality. He did not call it that, of course, but in our conversation one day about this friend-of-my-sister's-friend and female cab driver he had become very fond of, he whispered in that loud way he did: *Bobbie, she no like the boys.*

I remember being momentarily perplexed and then simply accepting it. I could see the manly way she dressed and that her behavior was not particularly feminine. There was no judgment about it, it was just the way she was, we liked her and we all became fast friends. Papa continued to be in touch with Bobbie for many many years and came to know several gay women through her, all of whom he invited into his home and all of whom ended up calling him Papa. In fact, a small gay contingent was present at the services when he passed away and I was touched when I saw Bobbie cry.

Like many religions, Islam does not take a favorable position on homosexuality but here is Papa's independent thinking again. He was no fundamentalist. He was a realist in many ways and I think it showed most in his acceptance of others. Papa met the female taxi driver through one of Delilah's high school friends. There was an immediate attraction, you could hear it in the way they spoke to one another, in the many conversations they would have. Papa would call her when he needed a ride to the market or something and he would in turn invite her to our house for a home cooked meal. She would always say that she got a kick out of Papa and they teased one another back and forth. His comment about her preference made me feel that he somehow needed to explain her but he also would defend and protect her, just as if she were one of his own. She must've known that.

The True Story About Papa's Dentures

Had I known then what I came to understand, I would have been a great deal more concerned growing up the way I did. All I knew was that my father never backed down from anyone. Even though he was rather small, likely never exceeded 150 pounds, he was big and strong to me. Still, I am sure that there were times he paid for his "confident" attitude.

I once asked my father why he wore dentures; what had happened to his teeth, I wanted to know. He responded hesitantly. Mumbling something about a Jewish dentist, *one by one*, he explained, he lost his teeth. While he indeed may have been joking, I remember specifically feeling that Papa had unfortunately been a victim of poor dentistry, no matter the nationality of the accused professional. Since Papa had not made a habit of generalizing prejudices to an entire group, I thought it unlikely that the Jewish part was in any way pertinent. He may have, in fact, had a Jewish dentist, or perhaps 'Jewish' was simply thrown in for some added color to the tale.

Nonetheless, for a long time I felt hurt over this particular story. Many years later, I was speaking to my mother and happened to mention it to her. She looked a little puzzled and then said,

That's not what happened to your father's teeth.

What did happen, then? I asked. Mom said that Papa had been arguing with some rather large guy and as a result of one of the punches, a couple of Papa's teeth became loose. He then saw the dentist, who decided to extract them rather than save them. Then, for some reason, it was only a matter of time before the rest of the teeth had to be pulled. Mom said perhaps it was inevitable; Papa's teeth had not been in the best of condition. Well, I thought, that is interesting. Papa told me only part of the story. The part that would not damage his stalwart reputation in the eyes of one of his adoring daughters.

Of course, no matter what my child's perspective, Papa never made any claims to fearlessness, he merely presented himself that way, at least to us as kids. He had to sense some trepidation leaving his country at the young age of around 20 to make a new life for himself. He must have experienced some fear when he first came to the U.S. not even knowing the language. There is little doubt that he had to be somewhat terrified when he was faced with raising four girls and a boy in a culture that was very different from his. To say nothing of the fact that such undertaking was virtually unheard of at the time, even amongst most American fathers. And he had to be afraid when he found himself engaged in verbal battle with men much bigger than he—unfortunately, this happened a few times—when he felt no choice but to behave courageously.

It was important to Papa that his children adopt a similar attitude and he made a concerted effort to foster confidence in each of us. Perhaps it was because of what he said and what I believed to be true that I saw my father's actions precipitated by what he wanted, not feared, for himself and for his children. There is that big difference, coming from desire rather than fear, when speaking on how one is moved to act.

Raising Four Daughters

It might not be surprising to hear that there were awkward occurrences in the life of a single Arabic Islamic father raising four daughters. The one aspect of child rearing with which Papa encountered great difficulty was puberty. He had been dealing with an awful lot here, though. It had to be the worst of all possible combinations, especially given that there was no way out of 'life encounters of the female kind.' Mom would not be there to do the customary introduction on menstruation, which would undoubtedly rear its inevitable head. What then, would he do? How would he handle it? It is quite certain that Papa did not look forward to the day when his eldest daughter would approach him with anything having to do with that female stuff, let alone how his daughter had to feel! Nonetheless, she would have to ask for money. And Papa always demanded an explanation whenever he was approached for money.

I remember the day because I was about as anxious as was my sister, while I made the pathetic choice to listen from behind my bedroom door. After a few start and stop attempts to explain, a frustrated and exasperated Delilah finally blurted:

I need 50 cents Papa.

She held out her hand. And that was it. Papa never said a word. Perhaps he was rendered speechless with embarrassment. After he reached into his pocket and handed Delilah more than she asked for, she took off running in the direction of Jackie's store in a certain state of complete humiliation. After that, all that any of us daughters ever had to do is ask for fifty cents, and there were no questions asked. Still, we never abused the convenience.

I figured it was just fine that my sister had to pave the way. It was her firstborn right, after all. I was only too happy to be spared the "privilege." But I did understand how difficult that had to have been for her, especially since she was still attempting to recover from the whole idea in the first place with very little preparation, introduction, or fanfare into womanhood.

At a fairly young age, I was made aware of the distinction in the Arabic culture between male and female. It was conspicuously a man's world, and that did not seem to matter much or to cause any great anxiety for me and my siblings, even as it is true that we had no choice. Papa was *Abu el Banat*, the father of daughters, and only when I realized that there was a kind of humiliation attached to an Arab who fathers girls rather than boys, it became much more difficult to accept. It was then that I had grown to understand and appreciate Papa's position in our lives. His insistence to be granted custody of his female children and his belief that he could do it without the help of a woman or any system. He never backed down and his children could hardly have acknowledged all that he was dealing with.

The gender distinction plays out in a fairly widespread custom in the Arab world as people tend to dress a boy like a girl for the first five years of his life. This is intended to counter the possible harm of belief in an "evil eye"—that wicked influence coming from one who has ill intentions. Since there is more reason to be envious of a little boy than a less-valued girl, dressing him as such would likely reduce the chances of his falling victim to such endangerment.

Perhaps Papa had become more "Americanized" than any of us ever thought. Although I can recall occasions of sexual distinction per se, there was not one moment in which I felt devalued by Papa because of my gender. Nor did any of my sisters. Perhaps this was all by design. He was either very much his own person, not bound by the routine conventions of his culture, or way ahead of his time.

When he was not working, Papa was at home with his kids. With each passing year, I grew more consciously aware that my father spent all of his waking hours, minus work, with his children. Later I considered that it had to be difficult to be so selfless. I knew my father thoroughly enjoyed the company of the opposite sex, yet he never brought a woman home nor did he carry on any relationship of which we were aware. In fact, he stayed legally married to our mother until the day he died.

Papa's equivalent of a night out with the boys was attending meetings at the Yemenite Benevolent Association in Lackawanna, near the steel plant. The members met in a large hall on the first floor of an old brick building. It was their way of remaining in close touch with each other and of maintaining a network. They would smoke, speak loudly and play cards. Often when we were still quite young, my sisters and I would get up on a small, elevated stage and while music played, the men would place coins on the floor nearby in exchange for our dances of entertainment. These were not sexy dances, we were just fully clothed little girls but I guess they liked it and thought it was cute. Still, it was our meager attempt to mimic the belly dancers that danced to the Arabic music we had seen on a number of occasions at various social affairs. Whether by desire or necessity, Papa had us accompany him to these gatherings. Not that I appreciated it at the time, but that is where I was able to pick up more of the Arabic language. The men there rarely spoke English, even if they knew it. At the club, with men speaking Arabic and playing cards in a heavy cloud of smoke, you could feel totally separate from the outside American world.

Romance & Other Nonsense

Although Papa's reserve precluded lengthy overt discussions on issues related to sex and the single girl, his attitudes and beliefs were not without disclosure and true to form, very sensible. About predicting a guy's behavior in a relationship, it was simple. *Watch how he treats his parents*, particularly his Mom. At first, I considered any advice on the subject to be tainted by Papa's desire to entirely distract his four daughters from men. As time went on, however, I would smile, even laugh aloud sometimes at some of the things he said that now seem all too true.

On marriage itself, Papa also kept it simple. *You are (in) love?* That was the question. Funny how that did not seem consistent with the Arabs' arrangement philosophy. Nonetheless, *if you are love*, then he would expect that you marry. Courtship was not condoned, particularly lengthy courtship where undoubtedly things can get out of hand, sexually, I assumed. Again, where Papa came from, marriage is the only way for a man and a woman to have a relationship.

Other than how I observed him being with my own mother, he held a rather clear-cut approach to the idea of love and marriage. We never spoke of romance and when it was inferred or when viewed on television, Papa mocked the over-the-top *I will die if I can't have you* as if it were a foolish concept.

Liking someone for how they were, respecting that person, was far more important than silly romance to Papa. That's the only thing that made the notion of arranged marriages understandable to me. In fact, all the arranged marriages that I was exposed to as a child almost appeared to take those things into consideration. I would characterize the couples as partners in life; definitely similar in values and belief systems. Temperament never mattered too much, because there was never any question as to what the house rules were with clearly defined roles for all. Gender roles are specified; there is little room for confusion and perhaps once the situation is fully accepted, there is little to argue about. With time, and after I had experienced a number of challenging "romantic" relationships myself, I was able to see the merit in the arrangements of my father's culture.

The "Amrikan System"

Papa's like/dislike relationship with his United States was often entertaining, but there were times when I posed the question about his desire to live out his life here. He would respond: *Whatta yagonna do? Too late go back now.*

Once Papa and I got into a discussion about his intention to take his five children to his country while we were all still very young. That was difficult, he said, due to conditions in Yemen, that most Yemenis leave their homeland, exacerbating the already challenging economic and social development of the country, which evidently continues to this day. He told me about how his people had been migrating west since the opening of the Suez Canal in 1869. Many came from what used to be the British crown colony of Aden before 1967. People were motivated to leave, he said, because of the extreme poverty that had been worsened by British imperialism. That was the reason, he explained, why his passport noted British for his nationality and why he had left his homeland to travel via ship finally arriving in America for the opportunity to work, earn a decent living and have a quality of life beyond that which he could have in his own country.

It was clear that Papa did not ever entirely let go, since he brought with him the family values of his land and insistently applied them in raising his children. Like his people, he demonstrated great pride for his heritage, maintaining a sense of duty and loyalty that must have guided him in caring for us without a wife. Like his people, he demonstrated tenacity and endurance in a way that could not be missed by anyone looking on at the huge task he had readily assumed when our mother left him with five small children. And like his people, he too was consistent with his ongoing remittance of monetary support to whatever family remained in Yemen. I know that Papa always missed his country, insisting on keeping informed almost daily of what went on politically and socially.

Arabic music played side by side with the Beatles and Rock N Roll at our house. Although pork and liquor were the two consumable products not permitted in our home for the majority of our lives with Papa, he finally conceded to designating particular pots and pans. The pork was a huge concession when you consider that the pig is held as a dirty animal.

I was often frustrated by an inability to provide satisfying answers to many of my father's probing questions about the American ways. I am not even sure that he always drew appropriate distinctions about what was American versus Catholic versus some unique circumstance. I only know that I often had difficulty defending against his complaints. It was clear to me that his frame of reference was uncommon in our everyday world. But Papa had a way of taking things down to such a basic level that made his thinking seem logical and straightforward. You would say something, a worry, for example, and he would look incredulously at you, up close and eye to eye.

So What?

Or—*Whaddya gonna do?* He would say, encouraging simplification of thought and action. It's like, no big deal, *is it???* With his response, he caused me to consider that perhaps Americans or maybe it was Catholics, usually both—did tend to over-complicate things. Perhaps clarity is attained through simplicity in private life as well as in the outside world.

I have said that Papa grew old overnight once it became evident that he had lost his fight to stay on the job. From a chronological point of view, he was likely beyond the mandatory retirement age and had to succumb to the pressure to end his work life. Still, Papa thought that was another fault of the "Amrikan System," that even if one chooses to work after retirement eligibility, they were penalized if they earned above some particular amount. The truth was even if he wanted to, Papa did not have an alternative to working at the plant. His working days would definitely end with Bethlehem Steel.

Death, a Practical Matter

Louie Penque was a family friend who taught me how to drive when I was sixteen. I thought of him as my American father. Louie treated me like a princess, taking me out to practice on his brand new Buick Electra 225. He said that if I could parallel park that big a vehicle I would be able to park any thing. He really liked Papa, defended his strict parenting and pointed out that that was why we were such "good kids." Although he never lived long enough after his late-in-life marriage to have children of his own, Louie enjoyed stories about Papa and always reinforced his values. He died on my sister Minnie's birthday, April 8th. The year was 1972. Papa was the one to deliver the news to me when I returned home from school one day: *You know who bass today?* He asked.

I had to think for a moment, the way I always did when Papa did not say a word just right. *Bass?* I asked slowly, giving myself time to decipher the meaning.

Yes, yes, muti, die, aiywa! Now he was bit annoyed with my failure to comprehend.

Oh, yes, Papa, who?

Louie Penque.

I sat down without taking off my coat, purse and books now sat in my lap. I could hardly believe it. He must have been late forties, early fifties, at most.

From what? I finally got out, trying desperately to digest this.

Heart-a-tak. And then a pause.

I didn't know the first thing about a heart attack other than it involved the heart and people did die because of it.

What ya gonna do? Papa muttered in the way that he only could, the way that said so much more than the words. He knew that I had great fondness for this man who remained single for a very long time to take care of his elderly mother and was always kind to us, taking us to eat after mass on many Sundays to the Pancake House downtown.

My father remained there, sitting in the silence with me for some time before the others arrived home.

Papa was matter of fact about death. It was the same when I attended my first wake with him. I was about 9 years old and I happened to be the one who was around and available. There is no prohibition in Islam on minimum age or gender to attend a wake or funeral so it is strictly up to the judgment of the parent(s). And with Papa we were always welcome to join him, in fact, he wanted us to come along, whenever visiting people or attending functions. Indeed he'd made it clear that his preference was to have as many of us who could or would join him. The man who had died was a countryman from Yemen. When Papa informed me of his death, I misunderstood. He said, *Ali Ibn Muhammad bah-ssed.*

The way my father always sounded P's like B's and A's like "ah's," I initially misunderstood and attempted to figure it out aloud, *He bust??* I said almost under my breath. And Papa, knowing that I got it wrong, said in Arabic *Mayit*, meaning the man died.

Whassa matter with you? He bantered, *You no understand English?* That was Papa's pat response to anyone not clear on what he had said in their language. It was usually not his pronunciation at cause for your confusion.

The wake was memorable. It looked like a bunch of Arab men—I do not remember any women—sitting around talking, while a phonograph played a prayer being sung in Arabic in the background.

I found out later that the audio backdrop were suras, verses from the Q'uran. Papa and I walked up to the casket, and he took his position at the head of the body. There was no kneeler. I just watched while saying a brief—Christian—prayer of my own. I was careful not to bless myself in the way of my Catholic faith, as the Arabs would not like that. First, with palms open, Papa whispered his prayer aloud. Then, he placed both palms over his eyes, and finally pressed his palms together.

That's it, he said quietly as he put his arm on my shoulder.

Bas, He's finished, and led me back to where the men were gathered.

Not long after, Papa received word that his dear American friend, Joe Corto, had suddenly died. I went to the funeral parlor with him once again. These people were Catholic and this time I noticed a kneeler on the side of the casket but I did not use it out of respect for my father. When Papa and I went up to pray, I watched him again. Everyone else watched too, as he prayed in his Islamic faith, over the body.

I was impressed. He remained true to his religion, proud and not hesitant to express himself, no matter how odd it may have looked to those present. After a short time, we walked out hand in hand and breaking the sad silence, I said:

You really liked Joe, didn't you, Papa?

Sure I like Joe. He was good man.

Then, after a few seconds, said almost as if he was thinking out loud, Papa continued in a low voice: *good man, bad man, we all gonna die some day*. I thought about how Papa would die one day and tried very hard to comprehend this thing called death when we never again get to see the face and hear the voice of the one we love. At least not while we're still here.

When our dog Duke had to be put to sleep finally after some twelve years with us, Papa was visibly crestfallen. In time, he had become a real pal to Papa, who boasted that Duke understood both English and Arabic, and with whom he shared daily morning coffee and toast.

We held on to our cherished German Shepherd for as long as we could, releasing him only once we felt it was more painful for him to stay. After the dog was finally gone, it was the same. *No more Duke*, Papa said, as we all sat on the porch watching a friend drive off with our beloved pet in the back seat of his station wagon. And that was that. Difficult for all of us, tearful and in great sadness, we all waved goodbye. Even through my tears I swear I could see the sadness in that beautiful dog's eyes. It was always Papa's response to death that has lingered with me. *Bas*, What is done here is done.

As tough and practical as I had always considered him to be, Papa was reassuring at the same time. I always felt as though I was in the presence of someone in control. Whenever I would get down, Papa had the common sense I was so in need of. He had that same matter-of-fact attitude about life as he had had about death. Life was definitely what you make of it, but of the things that were beyond our control? *That's the Life*! He would tell me, as he helped put things in perspective. Whaddya gonna do? Which I sometimes took as a resignation, but more often as a call to action.

Abundant Food

The preparation of food was a pleasurable pastime for Papa. And it was a good thing, too, since he had so many mouths to feed. As he went along, Papa taught us, or at least tried to teach us how to cook. Every dish had an Arabic flair of one kind or another, even when it was not an Arabic meal. He would methodically justify every step in the meal preparation process, carefully explaining the reasons for a specific ingredient or procedure.

Listen, he would say, *I tich you how you cook.*

Papa was always so proud about what he knew and how he could teach it.

He said he had learned on the ships as a Merchant Marine preparing for the masses, which was probably why it seemed he cooked in amounts enough to feed an army. Unfortunately, I never retained quite as much knowledge as did my sisters. I was voted least likely to succeed in the kitchen and developed a near aversion to domesticity.

Still, I absolutely adored his cooking, particularly the Arabic dishes. We all did. And actually, they were not all the mainstream "Lebanese" foods that are easily available today in the States, rather more the staples of the Yemenite people We had *Fetah* for breakfasts, which was unleavened bread with honey and melted simna—basically butter with spices—and a dish named *Ahseed*, which is a wonderful doughy substance served in a bowl with a dip cut out in the middle for the gravy. This was and is a dish intended to be eaten with one's hands. Papa always responded to our snickering about this by reminding us that we were not born with spoons and forks.

There was a lamb stew that Papa made that I have never seen duplicated, just as with his lentil soup. But there were regular American-type dishes he served also. The way Papa made steaks on the stovetop, sautéing with butter and onions made you feel like you were sitting down to a feast every time. Or the way he prepared chicken soup, first killing the chicken himself in our back yard, according to Islamic custom, then as he slow cooked the pieces, added the onions and celery and whatever else he did to make it taste like only Papa could. He even made sandwiches taste great, like the huge stack of tuna fish sandwiches he made with real mayonnaise, onions and celery for our lunches on school days on fresh slices of white bread. I can still taste and smell those sandwiches.

Papa always cooked with a number of vegetables, so it really was quite healthy. To this day, my sisters, brother and I still love brussel sprouts, Papa's favorite vegetable. I guess he taught us healthy eating because we still all eat like he fed us, save most of the Yemenite dishes, unfortunately.

As plentiful as the food was always at our home, more it seemed than a family our size could ever eat in one sitting, Papa would never sit down to eat with us. There was a time that I just figured it was because he had already eaten or that his schedule was irregular with his swing shifts at the plant. I think he might have even made it appear that way to us. But it turned out that neither was likely the case. Papa wanted everyone to eat first and allow themselves as much as they like and then whatever was left, he sat down to finish.

Often, in later days, when I came to visit, Papa would call out to me from the living room as I entered through the adjoining kitchen,

Yaa, Dolah, look what I make for you...in a voice that rewarded me for coming and enticed me into staying at the same time. It was fetah! I immediately took in the sweet aroma of the warm, sweet buttery unleavened bread in the pot with all my senses and heating it up atop the stove, I would go through that pot like I was storing up for a long cold winter, no matter what time it was or how hungry or not so hungry I happened to be at the time.

There is some reason to believe that Papa did not always take the time to be so resourceful in the kitchen. In the early fifties, when my mother was working part time and came down with a kidney infection, he was left with Delilah, the only child they had at the time. When my mother returned after a one and a half-month period, extended because she had been a non-compliant patient, she discovered two disappointments. The first was that Delilah hardly recognized her (children were not allowed to visit in hospitals back then) and the second was that she hardly recognized her own daughter because of the child's significant weight gain. When my mother inquired further into her diet, Papa explained that he had fed Delilah mashed potatoes with of course, lots of milk and butter. I guess there were not many options for feeding a one-year-old child. Still, whether it was that, expedience or just that he found something his daughter liked, a tiny toddler had become a chubby one for having been fed a regular diet of mashed potatoes for six weeks.

Food unfortunately became a likely source of comfort to us four girls, however, because we spent some time weighing more than we ought to. Like many families, we had a secret, or thought we had. Interacting with the outside world, we children operated somewhere between pride, family honor and lack of disclosure on the topic of our family status. We learned to keep a silence; it's not that we lied, we just didn't say what was too embarrassing to tell. Instead we may have sought comfort in filling that void of non-expression with food that was conveniently and abundantly available in Papa's household. What today might have meant that we had access to school or even widely accepted private counseling where we could openly discuss our sadness and confusions, we girls struggled with our weight as we attempted to avoid talking and stuffed our feelings.

But Papa would never see our weight as a concern, referring to the size of his daughters as healthy and a few other girls and women as *too skeeny*. He had more important things on which he preferred to focus, like his thing about watching out for the friends we chose and not talking to boys—ever.

Laughing with Papa

His generally quiet and reserved manner often gave in to a legendary sense of humor, poking fun at our individual frailties and breaking into thunderous laughter. We could not help but laugh right along with Papa, trusting his intent was non-malicious and that we were being reminded to not take ourselves too seriously.

For one, he had a thing with names. When our second dog, a Shepherd Collie mix, joined our family sometime after Duke was gone, Papa ended up naming him *Doodie* because my sisters kept talking about the dog doing "his duty." When Delilah's friend Judy called him once to report that a flat tire on her car would prevent her from taking him to the Broadway Market for his weekly shopping experience, he renamed her *Flat Tire* and never called her Judy again. Papa mischievously gave Maryann Lukonitis, the pretty dimple-cheeked Greek girl in our neighborhood, the name *Twist* because of the seductive way in which she walked. And, Jean, my brother's wife, would only be called by her middle name Elizabeth, because Papa thought Jean sounded much too close to "Jinn," which in Arabic has to do with the devil. In fact, Papa often had trouble understanding American names. He would ask, *What kind name that?* No one would bother to tell him that his distress was more often a function of his erroneous pronunciation of the word. Whenever he could not pronounce it, he just said it his way, so that my girlfriend Marlene was Molly, Krys was a two-syllable "Kurus," Pam was Bum and Paul was Ball. No one corrected him either, except his children at first and then finally would give up, realizing that most people just did not mind being temporarily renamed.

Papa rarely knew he was being comical. Even when he was serious he was funny. Becoming annoyed with how I stirred my dish of ice cream so that it was nearly liquid, he would say, *Il la yaa Dolah, if you want milk, get the milk*!

While he was genuinely annoyed at my preference for melted ice cream, I was consistently amused by his annoyance. He would often tease me, calling me *Rats* because of the way I picked at my food.

And he mimicked people. My mom when she ironed, because of the way she would place her tongue between her upper and lower teeth trying to concentrate, certain people, with the way they walked. He'd say, *Look, look, how he walk*, and he'd proceed the funny way he saw them walk. Or he warned his girls of the way some women walked, *You no walk like that*! And pointing to an example, *She walk bad*. When he told a story, he mimicked that way some people spoke, going from voice to voice, introducing it with, *And then he say*…and he would launch into the mimic of how he heard them.

My brother Ed recalls Papa's deliberate walk downtown to the Post Office that would often result in our goading him along as we went ahead at a faster pace and then he'd suddenly burst in to this quick paced walk, going much faster than our little legs could take us. Now he laughs and waits for us to catch up. It was a memory that demonstrated Papa's routine insertion of good humor.

And he did not exclude himself from the mix as he poked fun. He repeatedly told the story of how and why he decided to stop wearing his false teeth

I sneeze, and duk, the teeth, he come out, he explained as he gestured with a sweep of his hand toward the floor, until one day he just decided not to bother wearing the dentures anymore. It was the dentist who ordered these teeth who was to blame. He was *a shoemaker* disguised as a doctor. And after his cataract operation, my sister Minnie and I went along to the doctor with him on Delaware Avenue to pick up his prescribed eyeglasses. After wearing them for only a few minutes walking, he threw them down at the street. I believe that Papa finally discarded his bifocals for good after a few attempts to wear them for improved vision but his eyesight was worse with the glasses, he said. The eye doctor, *he shoemaker, too. Same same*. Papa loved to laugh, the uproar that would usually follow his exclamatory declaration of one thing or another.

We kids would laugh too, when he got frustrated or upset with one or more of us and used Arabic to express his frustration.

Gini! Laysh Gini Malahauck Ishreen Nafathuck! He enthusiastically called out on numerous occasions, meaning something about the devil doing something or other to us or causing us to do something that annoyed him.

Delilah tells a funny story about Jehovah's Witnesses coming to our door attempting to recruit followers as they do. Unlike most people who either sent them away or never answered their doors, Papa invited them into the house to tell their story, *so long*, he warned them, *as you listen to me tell you about how I believe after you finish.*

He listened, with undivided attentiveness, to all the missionaries had to say and accepted the Watchtower brochure they presented. After they completed their spiel, Papa took his turn telling them about Allah and the prophet, Mohamed. I don't know who had the floor longer but they did return Papa's respect and courtesies, remaining until he was complete, whether they were really interested or not.

Papa, the Catholic Church & Islam

Papa's concession to allow us to worship in our mother's Christian faith was a bigger deal than we all realized at the time. As a Moslem, Papa likely assumed that his children would follow in his faith. After all, it is the absolute belief of a Moslem that Islam is the only "correct" religion, although other faiths hold similar claims. Papa believed this as it was stated in the Q'uran, the Holy Book of Islam, the thirty divisions—juz—separated into four sections, all received by only one man, the prophet Mohamed, unlike the Bible, during a 23-year period. Papa said that God had selected this man, an illiterate orphan, born in 570 AD in Mecca, known to be *al ameen*, the honest one, the trustworthy, to inform His people of *el hak*, the truth. He spoke passionately about how Mohamed's father had died while he was still in his mother's womb and about when he was only six years of age his mother passed away. Papa was as serious about his religion as any Islamic Arab; indeed the religion and the culture are inexorably linked.

Papa prayed facing the east to Mecca five times a day and never gambled, ate pork or drank liquor and when he was older, he simply prayed lying down. Ingesting pork was *wesach*, dirty, and meant that you were exposing your health to disease. To drink, or to be *sakran*, was tantamount to losing your mind, in which case you are rendered useless and no better than the animals who were not given the ability of the mind to think clearly, unencumbered by the evils of consuming alcohol. These ideas were unheard of by the American Catholics who comprised the majority in our circle of friends, helping to form our frame of reference outside our home.

Papa thought the Christians had it all wrong because he sees we pray to statues. When he asked me what we did when we went to church, I felt like he already knew the answer and wanted to trick me into telling him so that I could hear from my own mouth and come to see it his way—how silly it was that we needed "symbols" to represent a God who can not possibly be made into an image.

When you go to church, how you pray?

Whad'd you mean?

I mean, when you go to church, who you pray to?

To God!

You pray to God, or you pray to statue?

To God.

What about the statue, you look at statue, you say, God, give me what I want, give me what I need? He persisted.

I was perplexed. *No.*

Allah is here, only one, he points upward. *He no in statue*!

I know, I assured him.

Papa considered statues in church as the idol worship of pagans, that which Islam, his religion, sought to replace, or at least correct.

I was only seven years old, how could I clearly understand the distinction? But Papa's prodding and questions got me thinking.

******

Islam is a religion of tolerance, patience, moderation, wisdom, and compassion, but autocrats have given it a bad name by invoking the religion to justify unholy ends. Papa observed all Islamic holidays, and told us about the Archangel Gabriel, who appeared to the prophet Mohamed in his cave on Lailat-ul-Qadr, four days preceding the feast day of Eid, the great day that marks the end of fasting of Ramadan. Angel Gabriel delivered religious revelations to Mohamed, who was by this time forty-one years of age. Mohamed received his first revelation sitting on Mount Sinai near Mecca away from all worldly desires. I recall feeling comforted that Catholicism and Islam had at least had one angel in common.

Like all good Moslems, Papa believed in and abided by the 5 basic essentials of his religion. First, *schahada*, the belief in the unique existence of God and Mohamed as his last prophet. Next, observing the two opportunities for prayer: *salat*, the formal ritual, five times per day, facing east to Mecca: just after sunrise, noon, afternoon, after sunset and late in evening and, for religious activities, wherein the body should be as clean as the soul—technically one has to wash his hands and arms up to elbow, feet up to ankles, ears, nose, mouth must be rinsed and hair wet before entry into the Mosque.

One begins the prayer standing, palms up and heavenward, then they are put to the ears (a woman puts her hands to her breasts). Then one bows and puts one's hands on one's knees. After standing up again, one falls on one's knees, touches the ground with the forehead. Then from sitting position, one stands up again. These motions repeat throughout the prayer—which is a recital of verses from the Q'uran and the prayer ends in a kneeling position with one's hands raised to Allah. These religious practices become compulsory for girls 9-15 years of age, boys 12-15.

The third tenet implores believers to share their wealth by giving charitably (*zakat*). Papa interpreted this to mean that rather than select a few favorites, he would give just a little to every charity that solicited him and he kept this practice for the duration of his life. Fourth, a Moslem must fast during the month of Ramadan each day of the month, from sunrise to sunset, eating only once per day. There is no eating, drinking, smoking or engaging in sex between sunrise and sunset. Ramadan is defined by the Lunar calendar so each year there is a shift forward of 10 days, which means fasting may have to be done at the peak of the summer. And lastly, one needs to make *Haj*, a pilgrimage to Mecca, at least once in one's life.

Even from my young child's perspective, Papa's Islam seemed devoid of pretense or hypocrisy. In my earliest years of receiving the Holy Sacraments in the Roman Catholic faith, I saw inconsistencies that I questioned. Those who sought to assist me in my inquiry reminded me of the mysteries of faith, and pointed to Biblical references, to the bad things that happened to doubting Thomases. It felt almost like the Church used the fear of God to control its followers, but I never believed that was God's intention.

For as long as I can remember, I did not want to be afraid of God, only to love Him and to believe in Heaven, not a Hell. It made no sense to me to say that there was a "Supreme Being" who loved me unconditionally and at the same time would punish me and send me into everlasting fire if I made a mistake. Although Islam spoke of the devil (jinn), it seemed to love more than fear God (Allah) and I heard the term "Paradise" more than I did the concept of eternal damnation or Satan. One is forgiven all his sins with a simple sincere declaration that *La Allah illah Allah*, there is no God but Allah and Mohamed is his messenger. Islam also appeared to be more inclusive and universal than the Roman Catholic faith, less formal and more about how to live. These were just my perceptions, but I know now that having had the experience of a dual religious background was good for me somehow as it broadened my understanding of the meaning of life.

Papa never pushed his religion in any overt way, and for that matter neither did my mother, other than requesting that we attend Mass on Sunday, which, remember, had been required by the schools we attended anyway. But Papa lived his beliefs, in self-surrender to God (which is what Islam actually means) and that was a far better model than any regular attendance of scheduled worship conducted in a particular building.

I might have felt differently had Papa ever said anything negative or dismissive about Jesus, because as far as I was concerned there was nothing to dislike about this great historical figure and holy man. But he did not. Rather, he made sense about Jesus, and spoke of him with reverence. He was a prophet, like Mohamed, and a very good man, born to Miriam, one of God's creations just as we all are. He did dismiss the concept of "Divinity," three persons in one God because

Allah wahad; *only one*. This was not a different God than my mother's God, the God of the Catholics, just their name for Him. Jesus was one of the three great messengers, divinely inspired, as was Moses and Mohamed, only he was not God.

Even now, I can see how the Islamic faith emerges powerful in its assertions because Mohamed was the last prophet or messenger, and it is guided by the Q'uran, a book that had theoretically been written in such a way as to guarantee that it came directly from God. It was given to his good and humble servant, Mohamed, all during his lifetime unlike the Bible, which was written and interpreted by many after the death of Jesus. In fact, because Allah spoke to Mohamed in Arabic when dictating the words of the holy Q'uran, believers pray only in Arabic. Mohamed was the last of the three great prophets because according to Islamic belief, he was chosen to bring to the world a correction of earlier corruption in humanity's knowledge of the truth. Its intent is to teach how people may live together in peace and harmony regardless of race, class, or beliefs, which sounds inclusive and corrective of mistakes made in the translation and original intentions of the other great messengers.

Papa had always been disturbed about the American media's biased portrayal and inferences of a theocratic society in the Arab regions. He explained that where people are predominately Islamic in beliefs (with Arabs actually forming only a small portion of worldwide believers), the culture is reflective of the religion, but that is because its spiritual underpinnings are about how to live and that was not bad. He thought that it was a mistake to hold the religion or an entire race responsible for the human actions of a few with political agendas. Indeed it is written in the Q'uran that if a man so much as kills one person he may as well have killed an army.

Even with definitive guidelines, there would be occasion for some commotion in my family because of the issues brought about by a dual culture and religion—particularly when the tenets were diametrically opposed to one another. For example, the Arabs essentially condone an eye-for-an-eye philosophy in maintaining law and order. This obviously runs counter to the Christian idealism of turning the other cheek. This was good, it made me think, rather than accept one way as the only way. Eventually I had to decide for myself and recognize value in each. It was not always easy of course, but I believe it contributed to making me a more balanced and open-minded adult.

In the end, I believe it was the similarities between the Islamic and Christian faiths that made it more palatable to us children caught between two religious worlds. The belief in one God and in living a good moral life here on earth with the promise of salvation in the hereafter were two strong common denominators that were reinforcing and offered the consistency we seemed to need.

With both faiths being rather ritualistic, religion was felt dramatically in our lives. Where Catholics had us going regularly to confession to tell our sins to a priest, the Muslims embark on the Haj to Mecca. A functional difference to be sure, but the objective is the same: to absolve oneself of his sins in preparation for entry into God's kingdom.

Catholicism eventually proved to be a more practical religion for me and my sisters and brother, but Papa remained fiercely loyal to Islam. Even today, my sisters and brother remain rather good Catholics and of Papa's ten grandchildren, all except three have been raised Catholic. Speaking with them on occasion about this, I get the sense that other than the recognition of Papa's faith, they never felt one way or the other about it, only that there was little sharing or common ground with him on religion. There was a mutual respect about it and they are intelligent enough not to condemn Islam because of the anomalies evident in some of our current events.

I have pursued other religions and practices. I recognize that there are many paths to God and I choose a particular belief and continue to read and seek.

A few years before he died, Papa paid to have someone make his pilgrimage, the Haj, to the Kaa'ba by proxy. The Kaaba is the cubical stone structure covered with cloth and stands in the middle of the Masjid al-Haram in Mecca. It is revered as the House of God, which is why Muslims direct their prayers toward it five times a day and why in Mosques across the world, the Giblah, or altar, is positioned in the direction of Mecca.

Being a bit of a skeptic when it came to untenable exchanges of money, I asked a lot of questions about the paper verification on this Haj by proxy and thought it curious that Papa felt so strongly about the meaning of such a symbolic exercise. He felt unable to make the trip himself and it was his final outstanding obligation.

Before I die, yaa Dolah. I no can make it myself, he reminded me.

I'll take you, I said, excited for the moment while I still believed it could happen.

How I gon' go? Different now over there.

Well yeah, I thought, a place does change after 40 or 50 years.

I no see anyway, he added. Papa had questioned his vision for many years and now he was resigned to not being comfortable with the degree of sight he had left. Papa would not budge. Once again, he had the last word.

The nuns who taught us had been aware that Papa was a Moslem. He made a point to explain all that as soon as he met them. It was not always easy for them to understand what he was saying, but they liked Papa and Papa liked *the sistas*. They maintained a mutual respect for one another for all the years it took all five of us to graduate twelve years of education.

Apart from the difference in faiths, the basic beliefs, values and philosophies of the nuns were similar to Papa's. They enjoyed having his children in class and enjoyed his verbal teasing on occasion. We were obedient, respectful and usually performed in an academically acceptable, if not superior, fashion. Our mother played a role also, as she frequently reinforced the importance of classroom discipline, academic achievement, respect for our teachers and all those in authority.

Both my parents taught us these qualities by example, but they were also very direct when they felt that was necessary. Mom even used a threatening approach when it came to behaving for our authority figures. *Don't you dare* (misbehave)! And she took religion and its fear-based dogma literally, causing her to be more insistent and using it to fortify her rationale.

Respect was one of those tenets that had been continually stressed as we were growing up. Authority figures earned your respect, and to show disrespect was absolutely unacceptable by both our parents.

Papa met and spoke to the nuns only a few times before there was no doubt their disciplinary tactics coincided and reinforced his own, so in many ways we were the perfect school children. We never gave anyone any trouble. These standards did not appear to be out of line with our friends' parents, either. In those days when a child was disciplined in school, it was generally understood that the parent would support the authorities and professionals.

As far as Papa was concerned, there was a clear correlation between respect for others and self-respect. He said that self-respect allows one to respect others and to command respect for himself. It used to drive me crazy when he repeatedly demanded, *Respect yourself, Yaa Dolah!* It was too vague a term for me in my early years and the command sounded so all encompassing and ominous. I knew that it was a highly regarded personal quality in Papa's culture; I just think I was a bit afraid of it. Did I have it? Will I always? Could I live up to its expectations? How could I be sure that I would not fall off the self-respecting bandwagon? It is honor, dignity, pride, and always proper behavior.

Like most children, my siblings and I always wanted to behave in a way Papa could be proud. Self-respect and family honor were highly valued. Admittedly, there was some pressure on us, especially us four girls to "perform" in such a way as to not violate this very dominant characteristic requirement. With the preoccupation of the self-respect issue came the acknowledgement of duty on the part of Arabic women, daughters and sisters to behave in a sexually ethical and appropriate manner. While my sisters were unquestionably dutiful, Papa kept extra tabs on me, about whom he could never be certain. Oddly, and perhaps even in protest of the distinction, I chose not to defend myself against it.

A Reason to Celebrate

Besides his disciplinary tactics and strong religious and cultural beliefs, there was something else Papa was consistent about. Perhaps only for the sake of his children, he made a big deal and created much tradition around American holidays but that could have been because Mom was present and involved with us during these festive occasions.

In many respects, Papa adopted his Amrikan System. Or, perhaps he acclimated to some of its ways, if even reluctantly so and if only for the sake of his family. Just as he allowed us to attend church on Sundays with our mother, he celebrated Christmas with us in the Christian fashion. Each year we had a tree under which sat a Nativity Scene, inviting the entire commercialization aspect into our home.

We had costumes on Halloween, so that we could go trick-or-treating like all our friends. Easter was celebrated with baskets filled with chocolate, most of which Mom purchased, but Papa contributed as he saw the need, usually for food and sometimes new shoes or dress outfits for the occasion.

Every year just before Thanksgiving, Mom would come over, ask Papa for a certain amount of money for the turkey and all the other stuff that she believed was tradition for the holiday, and he willingly handed it over. When it came to food, there was never too much resistance on Papa's end. It was as if she could make up any number and as long as it was to feed the family; he never gave her a hard time. Mom would begin preparations the night before and the festivities would last well into the next night on Thanksgiving Day. We always had the biggest turkey money could buy with all the trimmings. It was the one time each year that we could count on Mom to be with us for the entire day. Papa would roll out the red carpet and make it very easy for Mom to be there and even sleep over if she wanted. Thanksgiving was a special holiday because we all spent the whole day together, sat down to eat as a family and give thanks, but for us holidays were memorable particularly because they were days when we could almost feel like a normal family.

One Mother's Day, we had all convinced Papa to buy a Cupid statue plant holder from Maisel's furniture store as a gift to our Mother. It looked like a Roman art piece and stood about three-foot tall. We knew how much Mom wanted it, but it was expensive and Papa had to be convinced that it was worth it.

On that Sunday, the five of us prepared for her arrival. We were all very excited about the surprise Mother's Day present. When Mom came to the door, Papa went to open it while we children hid in anxious anticipation behind a door in the hall. We wanted to catch her reaction, and then all come barreling out from behind the door. It was to be a magical celebration and reunion.

After a few moments, Papa said *Habby Mother Day* and handed Mom the gift-wrapped statue. As she pulled off the paper, she looked around and asked where the kids were. Then beholding her coveted statue, she sighed happily, gave Papa a kiss on the cheek. *Thank you, Saleh.*

I recall being very excited about that kiss, which I was readily willing to misinterpret. But, that was it. She could not stay because she had something to do. In fact, she left the statue behind and said that she would pick it up later.

Of course, Papa seemed a little disappointed but I think he was used to it by this time. We probably all were. He had busied himself with making a living and taking care of his family and had a full if not distracted life. And mom was not focused on, likely unaware of how much it meant to us. Our dashed hopes of this providing some encouragement for her to return to remake a family was not something she likely ever even knew about as no one would dare mention it. Just an idealistic pipe dream of a bunch of children and their hopelessly optimistic father. Oddly, no one, including mom, other than me remembered the event all that much except to say that there never was much hope once mom left so expectation was minimal.

Still, if I had to point to one moment, this would be the day I gave up on my dream of having my family reunited, happy and intact, normal. I told myself that we could not make things happen just by wishing it to be and that expecting things could very well lead to big disappointment. I learned to have no emotional investment in outcomes, and I built a wall, refusing to give in to my sad feelings, understanding that it is a bad thing.

But mom is definitely sentimental. Many years later, when we were all in our teens and mom was in the hospital for her hysterectomy, we had all planned to come visit her and bring her flowers. We chose a yellow vase and had the florist place a variety of flowers in, creating a full colorful bouquet. The attached card read: *Mom, you always wanted flowers, now here they are*. It was signed by all of us and Papa. Mom still has that vase in her dining room and has kept the card all these years in a special place.

It was really towards the end of my father's life that I would finally understand how my father had loved my mother our whole lives. One day the five of us were at the hospital with Papa as he lay in a semi-conscious state and one of us, hearing someone coming down the hall, mentioned that *Mom is here*. Papa's eyebrows lifted, as he struggled with a benign smile. *Unbelievable*, I thought, as I fought back tears. *He still loves her*.

That day, I knew what unconditional love really looks like. And although my father never was able to get my mother to come back to him and our family, the love he held in his heart for her was a good thing.

Papa especially loved parades. On St. Patrick's Day, he would gather us together for a trip downtown to view the parade. We went early enough to get a good spot and always stayed until the very end. Papa enjoyed all the marching and the music, particularly the bagpipes. One would think he really did have some Irish in him that day, as he'd insist on having us delight right along with him in the loud display of scotch-plaid jangle of the bagpipes he so loved.

Papa loved the patriotic holidays, as well, and celebrated his patriotism as if he was a native. So that Memorial Day, Veteran's and Labor Day were each marked with the American flag, a way to show his patriotism and gratitude to the country he now loved and lived in longer than he had his native land.

Oddly enough, Papa's favorite holiday was the fourth of July. It seemed to bring out the child in him for some reason. He beamed as he carefully doled out the fireworks that he had purchased well in advance. He called them *firecrackers*, a little bit at a time to each of us five and selected close friends, beginning a few days before the fourth. We never knew what his total supply was because he had a secret hiding place that no one dared search out. On the fourth most everything was revealed for use. Papa saved a few sparklers for the days that followed as a surprise after our individual supplies had all been spent.

It became a family tradition to watch the televised events in Times Square in New York City every December 31st. After we had all gotten old enough and were no longer living home, the tradition transferred to a phone call at midnight, no matter where we were. Each of us would get to a phone as quickly as possible and call Papa to wish him a Happy New Year. Before long, Papa formed a contest by announcing what number caller (one through five, for his children only) you were. He would answer the phone: *Happy New Year to you, number 2, number 4, etc...* It was always so frustrating to be at a public place that night and have to wait in line for the phone to be free around the midnight hour, preventing you from being Papa's *number one* caller.

One very special December 31st, I had been dating a gentleman who liked my father very much and suggested that we spend the evening with him rather than go out. At midnight, we toasted in the New Year with a cup of tea. Papa really enjoyed it. I thought it was real sweet that this boyfriend cared to do this since it was likely that it was one of the driest holidays Tim had ever had.

Today, to carry on this family tradition since Papa's death, my mother, sisters, brother and I continue to call one another at midnight on New Year's Eve. Nonetheless, we all dearly miss the phone call to Papa that would usher in the next year.

I have often wondered if Papa's willingness to assimilate despite his inherent resistance to the *Amrikan System* were attempts, after all, to compensate for the loss he perceived his children to bear. It was tough enough for us, so why not allow for some enjoyment on the most celebrated American holidays. Or perhaps he started out with a tolerant nature and merely decided to participate with enjoyment while he was at it. As much as I like to suggest that Papa had been "Americanized," however, there was too much evidence to the contrary. He did what he did for his family.

A Pragmatist

Papa's seemingly unlimited expenditures on food, especially during the holidays, were in stark contrast to his unyielding pragmatism when it came to clothing. Almost without fail, Mom could be expected to approach it the same way.

I need money to buy the children clothes and shoes.

The red flag was waved.

What? Papa would ask incredulously. *What they need*? *They have clothes, lots clothes*. *Here*, he'd say as he pointed to an open closet door or a bedroom chest of drawers, proving his point, *What's this???*

Papa never understood, as did Mom, why anyone would buy more than one pair of shoes, or has to have a dress coat *and* a casual coat.

Why you need more than one? He often inquired.

Sometimes Mom's frustrations would simply make her leave in a huff, still feeling responsible and obligated to buy what she and we thought we needed, or wanted.

Papa did not always approve of Mom's expenditures on keeping us well dressed and updated, which because of her insistence on shopping at the finest stores, he usually considered excessive.

Look at these closets, they full clothes!

Still, she did manage to have all five of us in new outfits from head to toe each major holiday and on the first day of school every year. She also went to bat for us whenever there was a particular school celebration or event being held, explaining as best she could to Papa that we "(had) to go." He usually gave in and she usually left exasperated; she had to fight so hard. I always wondered why Papa gave us all such a hard time if in the end he was going to give in. But despite all she could and did afford for us, Mom had definite financial limitations, which, in the end, left her financially dependent on Papa when it came to many of the "extras."

Papa was strictly non-materialistic, therefore our lifestyle was modest, whether we liked it or not, whether it had to be or not. He was unattached, pragmatic and frugal, even manifesting in his crude fix-up concoctions around the house and yard, which may not have looked very pretty but always managed to get the job done. Money was for the express *needs* of the family, to send some *back home* to his native country, and the small "you-never-know-what-can-happen" savings. The unfortunate fact was that he only half-trusted the banks (the Depression experience could have been a contributing factor). That meant only some of what little Papa had was saved in a bank; the rest was somewhere at home, in sport coat pockets, under mattresses. His philosophy about one's work life was to make a good living but be *reasonable*. Time spent working and pursuing money needs to be balanced with treasured time for family. He was more concerned about time to visit people, conversation, connection to others and laughter. Spend money wisely, he taught us; you can always want so much more than you could possibly ever enjoy.

That's probably why, when it came to cleaning the house, which once Mom left, usually only took place when the house was in a really bad state and we would become zealous in our need to get everything back to being presentable, Papa's pat response was, *Never mind, just shine 'em up*!

Which meant simply to make the place look good or more accurately, good enough. He thought we got carried away in our attempts as we moved furniture, cleaned walls, and scrubbed floors. It became the household joke whenever one of us decided that we could not stand it any longer and began ordering the others to cooperate. It did not change our minds any, but it did add levity—something very needed during those times, and something we could always count on Papa for.

I remember a time when Papa first came to visit me at the home I bought about a year after I was married. He sat in my sunroom and looked out at my large backyard and said:

Like park over here; you no need go anyplace. Just stay right here.

And later, after he had called a few times only to repeatedly get my answering machine, he left a message: *What for you have nice home like that? You no stay home!? Wha's a matter with you*? We laughed upon hearing his frustrated voice but realized much later how that sentiment rang true.

Not unlike other parents and perhaps given our circumstance, it was probably inevitable that Papa was conscious of the need to love all his children equally. Today I have to consider that the love that he shared with us was equal in degree, but very unique to each one—as different as each of us and our needs were. The only proof I have of that is in the expression of a similar understanding amongst my siblings. Each of us had a "thing" with Papa. Something specific only to the individual, not to be substituted by any other. Even in our adult life, everyone had a designated 'assignment' during visits with him, which had the effect of making us feel particularly useful and special. Papa even had functional nicknames reserved that he resorted to when he wanted to make us laugh, such as *my hair cutter*, or *my back rubber*.

Even my husband had a job. He was somehow granted the distinct privilege of rubbing the powerful mentholated smelling Ben Gay on Papa's back each time he visited. The inevitable request would send shivers down Jack's spine as he would dutifully unscrew the cap and hold his breath, rushing to complete the rub down.

Come on, Papa, let's get going, he'd say, attempting to get it over with. Papa got a big kick out of that, admonishing him with, *Whassa matta with you, yaa Jack? Common, common, No smell bad, this Ben Gay! Good medicine!* He'd press the tube to his nostrils to prove his point and tease Jack.

See. Ahh, nice, as he inhaled just enough of the powerfully smelling cream, with his eyes closed, of course.

Saying Good-Bye

The ever-vigilant father, I believe that before Papa left this world, he was assured that his children were finally grown and able to care for themselves. Each of us had, by that time, someone in our lives for whom we cared very much, and whom Papa saw cared for us. I have to believe that he left with that comfort.

Papa died as quietly as he had lived. This time, he had been in the hospital for almost one month in a semi-comatose state. His condition of pneumonia had worsened, making hospitalization necessary. He had fought off so many ailments and this time it just seemed inevitable for him to give in and let go. My sister and I were to be at the hospital for our usual lunchtime visit, since the hospital was close to downtown where we both worked, but he never waited for us. Instead, I received the call that would remove me from a meeting and remain in my memory for all time. It was my husband, who after timidly dispensing with the bad news, asked me to remain at my workplace until he could drive the entire 40 minutes from his Niagara Falls office to take me to the hospital just a 10 minute drive away. This all meant that I was the last to arrive. My father was only the second person I had seen just after death. I entered the room, conscious of everyone's presence around the bed but seeing the face of no one, lay my head on his chest like I did so often, and thought to myself: *I hope you know how much you were loved.*

Papa died on a Wednesday, the first of December. His burial was essentially traditional with the exception of the extra time granted us for his wake. Traditional Arabic custom prohibits embalming, allowing about a 24 hour period to wake and bury the dead; we waked him an additional day and a half to accommodate our need to adjust and for our American friends. His burial would take place the following Saturday morning.

It is also custom that the directors not handle the body; instead, the body is dressed and anointed by Arabs, usually including an Imam (spiritual representative), in mummy-like fashion with new white sheets purchased especially for that purpose. Since I had not been this close to death in the Arabic tradition before, I was instructed step by step and had gone through the motions to buy the white sheets that would hold my father's body. The owner of the funeral parlor, already familiar with these practices, was nothing less than cooperative during the entire process. There would be no kneeler, so Christians prayed standing up just like the Moslems. The *fat-ha*, the opening verse of the Q'uran and other audiotape verses, *suras*, sang in the background throughout the wake.

Papa's casket had been reopened for the service at the Mosque. Inside the building, the men removed their shoes and were led in prayer. The Arab Muslims went first, the American men followed suit. Upstairs, all the women were able to look down upon Papa's open casket. It was the last time that I would see his body so I tried not to take my eyes off him. He looked so serene in his white garb and headdress. This is the moment I have dreaded for so long, I thought. The moment when his chest and his cheeks would forever be still.

I had a good view of him from the balcony where I was standing with the rest of the women. I remembered Papa telling me how it used to be that women were not permitted in the mosque and had to worship in their homes. The shoeless men, including any Americans brave enough to attend, were on the ground floor on their knees on small prayer carpets.

The harsh reality that began to settle in just as the mosque service was about to conclude was interrupted by the voice of a male relative of my father's. Directing his words to my teary eyes, he said, *You're father don't like it to see you and your sister cry*. I knew he was right and for the moment I could contain myself long enough to get to the cemetery. I recalled Papa's matter-of-fact attitude about death, that when *it's bas, finished* that's it.

At the cemetery, a few prayers were said by one of the Arabic men. Papa's only son, our brother, joined the other men in lowering the casket into the ground. All the while, they chanted, *La Allah Illa Allah* (There is no God but Allah) repeatedly. Once it was down, they began to take turns shoveling the dirt to bury the casket. This rather dramatic display seemed almost in contrast to Papa's unimpassioned view of death.

During this time of Papa's passing, there were a number of people who came to pay their respects. There were folks from the old neighborhood, friends, those with whom the five of us had worked over the years, and a cadre of Arabs from the local Mosque. I was touched by many, but by none so deeply as the first real *American* love of my life, Michael, the one my father had come to finally like but fell short of acceptance as a husband for his daughter. He sat there alone and in silence for a while, until I came to notice his presence. It had been years since I last saw him, but like many first loves, I thought of him often and could never forget him. There would always be a special place reserved in my heart just for him.

As he and I sat and talked for some time, he was busy making me laugh with stories and fond memories of the crazy times of our romance and the things my father did and said to get us to give our relationship the serious thought it deserved. Michael reminded me of one winter evening when he came to pick me up to go to the movies. Just as we were about to leave, Papa came hurriedly down the stairs to warn us of impending bad weather. He said that we *must not go*, because this was to be quite a destructive storm.

No go no place. It's trouble. I feel it, he had said.

At first, we considered that this may be a ploy to keep us close by and minimize the time we were to be alone. We had joked about it, saying that Papa's concern may have even had something to do with us traveling in a car sporting one cardboard window. Nonetheless, it was something about the way my father said, *I feel it* that scared my dear Michael. We decided to stay in, and there was, in fact, a bad ice storm that had occurred leaving a fairly significant destructive path.

At the funeral parlor that day, Michael explained that his interpretation of what Papa had said had little to do with the storm. He believed that Papa was, as he described, *a wise old guy*. In fact, he confessed to feeling that there was a prophetic quality in Papa's warning that evening. This, he assured me with all due respect, had been the only reason he had given in so quickly.

Coincidentally, Mom lost her job the same year in the same month that Papa passed away, leaving her depressed and financially challenged. The company that she had worked for decided to close up shop, which left many people, who like Mom, were already in their 50's and 60's. Because of the timing, however, I gave no thought, nor do I believe had most of us, to what Mom must have been going through. Years later when she explained how difficult life had become, I was surprised to learn how insensitive I obviously had been and how non-communicative my Mom had been about her troubles. She may not have felt entitled, and knowing Mom, she would not be one to ask for help. Still, I knew hearing of it that Papa would have taken care of her, just as he'd always done, making sure that she did not experience any dramatic hardships, particularly as it related to the necessities of food, clothing, or shelter.

Mom worked hard her entire life. She had been the "perfect employee" to all her employers—honest and trustworthy, dependable and hard-working, easy to get along with others and particularly conscientious. And for the majority of her work life, transportation was not easy, particularly during inclement weather. She took buses back and forth down Delaware Ave and then transferred to another bus down Swan Street. She worked the late shift so that she could remain available for us during the mornings and just after school. She never complained, really and we had little awareness of this sacrifice as far as I am concerned.

After a few years at Cadet Cleaners and around 1966, mom had seen an ad in the paper for work at Markel Electric and applied for it. She got the job and at first tried to work both jobs for the extra money she was excited to be able to make, but it only lasted a short time. She could not do it all and settled with the electric appliance company. Soon into her tenure at Markel, however, she became an inspector of heating and other appliances. Not long after that, she was offered the supervisor position; she had been recommended by the former "boss" who was returning to Germany. Mom said no at the time and did live to regret it, being supervised by a woman who was the company's second choice and as it happened, not so easy to work for.

Laid off from Markel after 17 years in 1982 when the plant closed and was sold, Mom received some money as a reward for her lengthy service but it was the same year that Stanley, mom's long time companion, lost his job. She recalls this time as one especially frightening and her most difficult year financially. Mom collected unemployment that year, standing in long lines alongside terminated employees of Papa's long time employer, Bethlehem Steel.

Doctors, Hospitals and Love

My father's religious beliefs were a constant source of strength to him during good and bad times. The couple of years before Papa passed away saw him sick too often. His lungs began to show the effects of cigarette smoking and exposure to the Steel Plant. There had also been evidence of tuberculosis with which he had come to this country a long time before. He began to experience even greater respiratory problems. It was inevitable that the medication would lead to side effects and the side effects at times seemed more noxious than the ailment itself.

To make matters worse, it continued to be a challenge to get Papa to agree to proper medical attention. It was well understood that Papa had no love for medicine and the entire medical industry.

Shoemakers, he repeatedly would claim, as he had so many times before. *They're all shoemakers!*

Hospitals were death factories to Papa. He never witnessed anyone who was better for having experienced a hospital stay. But I still believe that he knew how serious his condition was each time.

One night, I was awakened with a frightening phone call from one of my sisters fearfully conveying the seriousness of Papa's physical state. He had been running a dangerous temperature and needed to be taken to a hospital, but refused to go.

It took my husband and me at least 20 minutes to make the half-hour drive to Lackawanna, where he had been living after he was forced to leave Myrtle Avenue for an"eminent domain" consideration. As we arrived, throwing open the kitchen door to his house, Papa sat up directly onto his bed just long enough to announce:

I no finished yet! Looking up, and with his index finger to the ceiling, he said: *Allah, He know. I not ready yet.* Then, he ordered us. *Go home!*

None of us could believe that our father, burning with fever, would refuse help and then order us to leave. To be so certain that it was not yet *his time*. It was scary not to force him into the car and take him to the hospital, but we all managed to calm down long enough to consider his declarative statement, dramatic as it may have been. There was no doubt; he was not dying. Not yet. When it did come time for him to go, he was tired and ready. He left quietly and alone because he chose to. And there was that comfort that all of his children were finally able to go it without him.

Popular theory amongst some family members and friends is that our father was kept healthy and alive as long as he was because of his five children. (Papa's date of birth is actually unknown; official records were not kept in his village at the time he was born, but he was believed to be in his 80s when he died.) If there is truth to this, then there is something to be said for mind over matter and the self-fulfilling prophecy. Papa endured many serious accidents and ailments through the years. The Arabs insisted that his will to live had been governed by his need to meet his responsibility to his family.

Insh'allah, as Moslems say, *as God wills.*

Toward the end, on two separate occasions, Papa did become ill enough to be hospitalized, but he never went willingly. As his child, you could not help but feel like a traitor. Succumbing to medical treatment was always a struggle because of Papa's notorious indictment of the *shoemakers* and his general distaste of hospital facilities.

Admittedly, Papa never learned to be an easy patient. His tone of voice was sometimes offensive to those who did not understand him, which translated to a lot of people. The majority of the medical staff with whom he came in contact had also had difficulty with Papa's frequent obstruction of routine care as he gave the professionals a hard time about taking blood and giving shots. The numerous blood samples were often annoying to Papa, and after a while, seemed unnecessary and eventually annoyed all of us as well.

Since Papa hated gadgets attached to his arm, he often attempted to remove IVs, which only meant that we had to be on constant guard and convince Papa of their necessity. One physician, who had actually been a family acquaintance, called Papa a *cantankerous old fellow*, which we tried desperately not to take offense with. We did understand how one could get that impression.

I am sure that the language barrier added to my father's discomfort in the hospital. He often did not understand them and they made little effort to understand him. A family member was usually there to interpret both ways. Papa rarely took the medicine they prescribed, setting out to prove that they were wrong again. He would get better without it. In the hospital, he flirted with the nurses (usually in an effort to distract them from a procedure).

What you name?

You marry? He was asking about her marital status.

You look nice! As he took her hand and held it in a way that made her feel obligated to remain just a little to appease an old man.

Thank you, Mr. Saleh, Now you rest, Okay? She had to move on; nurses have busy schedules with many patients assigned to care for.

Papa often spoke to us in Arabic in their presence, especially when he did not want them to understand what he was saying. Sometimes it was a challenge not to laugh because of what he was saying, but Mom always stressed the import of politeness. Each of us had our own way of ensuring no one was offended.

When I looked back on those days in the hospital, I believe that Papa was frightened, that he would indeed rather die than be subjected to protracted stays at an institution or in a system in which he had no confidence. Growing dependence due to aging was not a comfortable state for a man who had managed more hurdles than I saw most anyone else's parent. He did not freely trust many doctors to begin with, and hospitalization under these circumstances is the most vulnerable of all situations. His daughters would therefore rarely leave his side; taking turns sleeping at the hospital (generally permitted when a language barrier exists). This was not easy, since we had jobs to report to in the mornings. But when it came to Papa, it was not something we took lightly; he so rarely asked anything of us.

Luckily, we all had very understanding superiors with whom we worked. One of the first times Papa was admitted to the hospital was over a blood count disorder. He was under suspicion for a contagious element and was in a private secluded room. This was the time I picked him up and forced him into my car with my sister Sinia. She sat in the back seat while he tugged at my clutch in protest. *Papa, my God, be careful*! I was terrified of the possibility of jerking us backwards on this uphill portion of the expressway. My sister and I felt really bad forcing the issue, but it had to be done, he was in trouble and the hematologist was waiting.

Sinia tells the story about one night when she was taking care of Papa during the time he was growing quite ill. He called her Saghema, the baby, or sometimes, Kufla, the name of his Aunt. Listening closely to him as he had a habit of whispering, not so loudly anymore, she leaned in toward him when he asked her to lie down behind him, as he often did with all of us once he became sick enough to be confined to his bed. Likely sensing her anxiety, he said, *I might die now but you no die with me.*

No, Papa, Sinia said, in the way we might dismiss discussion of a cruel reality. And she told him that day when he dies a part of her will be gone forever.

******

As pragmatic as he was about such major life issues, however, he was never quite the same after he had been forced into retirement. To make matters worse, the retirement occurred around the same time that Papa was forced to find somewhere else to live, as his long time residence on Myrtle Avenue was to be destroyed. Eminent domain was taking over the neighborhood. He chose Lackawanna for the obvious reason of returning to familiarity and to be nearby other Yemenites, but the move was disruptive and only added to his loneliness and feelings of despair. We were all just about independent by the time he made the move.

Lackawanna still has some Yemeni families living there today, but the area has pockets of deterioration as the homes are very affordable. There are a number of rental apartments in the vicinity and some folks fail to take care of their space. Papa's street was not one of the better ones, but he lived in a cottage behind another Arabic family who had several children and were like family to Papa. Their youngest, now around 28 years old, was the toddler who, after Papa passed away, kept pointing to an area by a tree in their yard repeatedly uttering the word *siti,* meaning grandfather and her mom explained that she believed that the dead show themselves to the young, mostly to reassure those left behind.

It was during this interval, after his move, that I became increasingly aware of his years. All of a sudden, it seemed, he was old. I did not recall being so consciously aware of his age while he was still working. Perhaps it was because I was too young then but I came to be much more sensitive about it. So did all my sisters and my brother.

One day, as I went to kiss Papa goodbye, I took his small face in my hands and looked into his little, hazy eyes. I always kissed him on his head, and then on his cheek, instead of both cheeks. I remember thinking about what someone had once said about a face telling a story. Papa had one of those long story faces. That was such a tough day. I knew that I could never be ready for Papa to go, but that was not something I would control. I never was any good at facing up square to things that were painful. So I simply would think of it no further. Or so I thought.

Then one day in the car, a familiar song was playing on the radio.

Singer Harry Chapin sang:

The leader of the band is tired, and his eyes are growing old...and his (song) is in my soul....I am a living legacy to the leader of the band...Thank you for the freedom when it came time for me to go; thank you for the kindness, and the times that you got tough. And, Papa, I don't think I said 'I love you' near enough...

The lyrics reminded me of how I felt that day in the house when I held his face in my hands. This was difficult for me, knowing that would become the song that would forever play in my head long after Papa was gone.

Happy All the Time

As Papa grew older, we tended to keep secret from him anything we believed would cause him emotional upset. I was married about four years before deciding it was time to have a child. It took about five months, but finally I became pregnant. Unfortunately, the pregnancy was ectopic and I lost the baby. After emergency surgery and a hospital stay of about six days, I had to recuperate in my home for an additional six weeks. During that time, I only spoke on the phone to my father. We had told him that I was not feeling well, and that the moment I was better, I would come to visit. After I finally arrived there one afternoon, Papa told me he had a dream that I had a baby. He told me it was a girl and that she was small, *very, very small.* In my astonishment, I was momentarily speechless. I knew that no one would have told him. I had to turn my face away in order to avoid having him see my eyes welling up with tears. But realizing that he may not live to ever see me have a child, I took the opportunity to ask a question for which I desired his answer. I asked him what name he liked for a baby.

As if he expected the question, he readily responded:

Basama, if it's a girl; Basam, if a boy.

Even though I wasn't particularly excited about the names, I asked why he chose those names.

Papa said: *Because, it's mean happy all the time.*

That conversation is one of my fondest adult memories with my father. Papa and I, alone together. He had held my hand while we talked. He was so happy to see me after that long time away.

Grieving

Within months of experiencing this trauma in my life, Papa would become ill enough that he would be forced to seek professional care once again, only this time it was terminal. It was not until this last time when Papa would be taken in that we became painfully aware of all that could go wrong in a hospital.

Since he was assigned to a "teaching floor," Papa was at the mercy of a number of practicing interns. This time he did not have a private room, but rather shared one with three other very ill, elderly men. The ward was located at the end of a corridor where a large window was often kept open. Since it was a chilly November and I repeatedly found Papa shivering, I asked why this was. I was told that once the floor was mopped, the air from the open window would help to dry it. Expedient housekeeping apparently took precedence over the comfort and well being of the patients.

There were a number of examples of inattention, carelessness, and what appeared to be a lack of sensitivity. I am sorry to say that I doubt this was an isolated incident or an exception. From what I have heard, many people have similar experiences and feel that same sense of helplessness that we did. I am sure that there is another side to tell, including excuses like short-staff conditions and the like, but far be it from me to side with the institution or the health professionals at the expense of a patient—this time, my own father. Even though my memory dims now with the passage of time and all of the details are somewhat sketchy, I cannot help but retain a negative image of Papa's final days in the hospital.

I think that I shall remember the day Papa died forever. In fact, I will never forget the phone call that would announce the incredible news and the excruciating wait from that moment until the time that I would arrive at the hospital. I remember Shakespeare's words often: *Love knows not its depth until the hour of separation.* I could never have been ready for Papa to go. I thought he wouldn't or couldn't and shouldn't, but maybe if he could talk to me, he would say, *I was ready, I was finished... Bas.*

At first, I was heavyhearted about the regrets that I have with my father. The times I left after only so brief a visit. I still hear him sometimes asking me, *you go so soon?* And I see his face; the way he looked at me. I try hard to keep my memory filled with all the good times, and the time I did spend with him.

Grieving was no stranger to me. Even long before Papa died, I grieved as that little girl who realized that her family was not like others. Papa could be the best father, but he could not be a mother, and he could not be *American.* I grieved when I got to high school and became aware of how insulated and sheltered a life I had lived. I never got to go to the Father-Daughter Dance in junior year, although I pretended up until the last minute that my father and I would be there. I even coaxed Papa to practice dancing with me on the kitchen floor. I grieved that night, too.

When I was in college, I took a class on aging as part of my psychology major. I recall writing a paper using my personal experiences. It was about then that I realized that I had never known Papa "young." I had seen pictures but I never knew him then, and I was sad. I felt cheated. I grieved for what I never had and felt sorry for myself.

Then, in my memory, I grieved while Papa was still alive. Over things he once was able to do and could do no longer. I remember thinking that he and I would never again take long walks, go to watch the parades downtown or enjoy shopping as a family to the Broadway Market. I would no longer delight at the sight of Papa at the skee ball machines that he loved to play so much at Glen Park and Crystal Beach. How he got such a kick out of winning us all those trinket ceramic banks. He'd always make sure he won things in numbers of five. And how he would *save them* so proudly in that special drawer, for God knows what. It had all been such a long time ago, but somehow I was feeling the loss as if it took place yesterday.

When Papa's health deteriorated, especially that last time, roles of father and child had reversed and it was clear that neither of us was comfortable in those positions. I can no longer remember how often I prayed for God to transfer the pain to me, I was so young and could handle it so much easier. It hardly seemed that he could be happy anymore, a man who was always so self-sufficient and proud. I thought a lot about how aging and illness can rob us of our dignity.

Celebrating Papa

There were an unusual number of warm, sunny days in Buffalo in the month of December 1982. I felt that somehow God had blessed the day we were to lay Papa to rest. Through the entire ordeal, I learned more about the customs of my father's people and discovered that there were only one or two local funeral parlors whose owners accommodated the Arabs, allowing them to proceed with custom without interference.

Forty days after Papa passed away, we held a banquet to celebrate his life, following another Arabic/Islamic custom. My family, with the help of many local Arabs, arranged to have the gathering take place in the hall beneath the Mosque.

Since this was our first time hosting, we relied on a few close friends and cousins to lead us through the process. As instructed, we had a gentleman go out to slaughter enough lamb to feed our many guests. The meat had to be fresh. The women assisted in the purchase of the rest of the meal. Several of the ladies would pre-cook the food at their homes, and deliver it to the hall.

We had bought enough food for more than enough people. When it comes to food, Arabs always think in abundance. As it turned out, I believe every Yemenite in the area came. It was announced, as usual, on the bulletin board at the men's club. Although there is no way to obtain exact counts with these folks, you could be sure that at minimum, eighty-five percent would attend.

When we arrived at the hall, it was a festive atmosphere. The men were back-to-back in the crowded kitchen stirring large pots of the pre-cooked lamb stew over the stoves. They grabbed my brother and husband who were expected to pitch in. The women were organizing the children on the floor in one section of the hall. They motioned for us to get settled in the area where my mother, sisters and I would be eating with all the women.

After all the men and boys were served, the women served the girls and then sat down to eat with us. As we looked around the hall, we talked about how Papa would be pleased. The two things he loved most in life were children and the sight of people sitting down to a hearty meal.

Precious Memories

Whatever it was that kept Papa alive as long as he was, I know that we remain grateful for the time we all had with him. And there were times we actually let him know that. I often verbally expressed my love to my father—mostly in Arabic. Papa would always respond with endearing phrases like *Allah-isalmak*, which literally means God protect you, or May God give you peace. He generally referred to his children in terms that in Arabic are wonderfully loving things to call someone, but are somewhat difficult to translate. One of my favorites was *yaa ei-nee*, meaning *my eyes*. But he never said the words "I love you" back to me, in Arabic or English.

I was in my twenties before I decided to ask Papa why this was so. He explained that it is not proper for a father to say to his daughter *Ana-be-hebak*, literally meaning "I love you," because it had more of a romantic connotation. I could not believe that he had never told me this before, allowing me to inappropriately use this phrase for so many years. Before I left that day, I asked Papa in English.

Papa, do you love me?

He said: *Why sure I love you!*

How much? I asked.

He replied, *I love you one million times one million.*

I believed him.

It seemed I had lamented more than I could have expected to in a lifetime. But after Papa died, I felt an ache that just stayed with me all the time. And as I attempted to adapt to the loss in my life, my mourning was subsumed in the solace of my thoughts as reflected in one of my journal entries from that time:

I cannot believe that I will never hold your hand again, or kiss your head. I will miss your laugh, your numerous and lengthy phone calls, and your long stories about the old country. I wish I would have asked more questions and listened more intently as you tried to tell me who you were. I want to remember the way you walked, talked, and laughed. I mostly want to remember everything you taught me. I will live with you forever in my heart.

I signed that entry: *I love you one million times one million.*